Joseph:
Not Your Ordinary Joe

Meditations on Joe and His God

RUTH ANN MOORE

Nancy Boring, editor

WESTBOW
PRESS®
A DIVISION OF THOMAS NELSON
& ZONDERVAN

Copyright © 2016 Ruth Ann Moore.
Photo Credit: Jeannie Manning

All rights reserved. No part of this book may be used or reproduced by any means, graphic, electronic, or mechanical, including photocopying, recording, taping or by any information storage retrieval system without the written permission of the author except in the case of brief quotations embodied in critical articles and reviews.

This book is a work of non-fiction. Unless otherwise noted, the author and the publisher make no explicit guarantees as to the accuracy of the information contained in this book and in some cases, names of people and places have been altered to protect their privacy.

Scripture taken from the Holy Bible, NEW INTERNATIONAL VERSION®. Copyright © 1973, 1978, 1984 by Biblica, Inc. All rights reserved worldwide. Used by permission. NEW INTERNATIONAL VERSION® and NIV® are registered trademarks of Biblica, Inc. Use of either trademark for the offering of goods or services requires the prior written consent of Biblica US, Inc.

Scripture quotations taken from the Holy Bible, New Living Translation, Copyright © 1996, 2004. Used by permission of Tyndale House Publishers, Inc., Wheaton, Illinois 60189. All rights reserved.
Scripture taken from the New King James Version. Copyright © 1979, 1980, 1982 by Thomas Nelson, Inc. Used by permission. All rights reserved.

Scripture taken from the King James Version of the Bible.

New Revised Standard Version Bible, copyright © 1989, Division of Christian Education of the National Council of the Churches of Christ in the United States of America. Used by permission. All rights reserved.

This World Is Not My Home (I'm Just Passing Thru), Albert E. Brumley (c) Arr. Copyright 1936. Renewed 1964 by Albert E. Brumley & Sons/SESAC (admin. By ClearBox Rights). All rights reserved. Used by permission.

WestBow Press books may be ordered through booksellers or by contacting:

WestBow Press
A Division of Thomas Nelson & Zondervan
1663 Liberty Drive
Bloomington, IN 47403
www.westbowpress.com
1 (866) 928-1240

Because of the dynamic nature of the Internet, any web addresses or links contained in this book may have changed since publication and may no longer be valid. The views expressed in this work are solely those of the author and do not necessarily reflect the views of the publisher, and the publisher hereby disclaims any responsibility for them.

Any people depicted in stock imagery provided by Thinkstock are models, and such images are being used for illustrative purposes only.
Certain stock imagery © Thinkstock.

ISBN: 978-1-5127-3544-4 (sc)
ISBN: 978-1-5127-3546-8 (hc)
ISBN: 978-1-5127-3545-1 (e)

Library of Congress Control Number: 2016904798

Print information available on the last page.

WestBow Press rev. date: 03/30/2016

Contents

Dedication vii
Acknowledgments ix
Introducing Joseph ben Jacob xi
Sold Genesis 39:1–6 1
Potiphar: Captain of the Palace Guard 3
Integrity: Joseph and Abimelech Genesis 20 5
Joseph: Integrity in the Face of Temptation 7
Suffering Joseph 9
Happy in Prison? Yes, Even There! 11
He's Not Listening 13
Potiphar Calmed Down Genesis 39:19–40:4 15
Joseph Paid Attention Genesis 40:1–23 17
Joseph and Jesus 19
Joseph and Jesus Parallels Chart 21
Samaria's Well John 4 22
Integrity Matters Genesis 40:20–23 24
Joe's Clothes Genesis 37:1–3 26
Joe's Clothes, Postscript Genesis 41:37–46a 29
From Tested to Teacher 31
All Things 33
Blessing Your Family 36
The Hand of God 39
Experiencing God Pharaoh Style Genesis 41 41
An Overnight Success Genesis 41:1–14 43
Journey Markers 45
Delight 47
Christmas with Joseph 49
Recipe for Prayer 51
Seventh Heaven 54
Go to Joseph 57

Don't Just Stand There!	59
Honestly! Genesis 42:6–26	61
Oh No! Genesis 42	63
It's Not about the Money	65
Relax!	67
Hospitality, Egyptian Style	70
Family Order	73
Joseph Shows Up	75
Rejected!	77
Psalm 95 Prayer	80
Family Respect	82
Together Again! Genesis 45:1–16	84
If by the Spirit	86
Standing Erect	88
The Laughter Link	90
Jacob and His God	92
Grace at Work	94
The Embrace of a Lifetime Genesis 46:29	96
The Remnant of Joseph Amos 5	98
Meanwhile	100
Joseph's Oath Genesis 47:27–31	102
He Sat Up in Bed Genesis 48	104
Appropriate Blessings Genesis 49	106
Blessing Primer	108
Faith of Our Fathers	110
Epilogue	115
Afterword: Resurrection, Joseph Style Genesis 45:4–8	117
Glossary	121
Works Cited	133

Dedication

To Bob—your wisdom and your patience are Joseph-like. God brings more good from your life than you can imagine.

Acknowledgments

Joseph: Not Your Ordinary Joe is the fruit of the prayers and encouragement of family and friends as I studied and shared what I learned over a two-year period. I am in your debt.

Special thanks to Nancy, my editor, for your insights and guidance.

Mom, your prayers mean the world to me. Thank you for your faithfulness and perseverance.

Patrick, my grandson, has endured more Nina (his name for his grandmother) lessons from Joseph than he would care to admit. You know my dreams for you! Thank you for drawing Joe's clothes.

You siblings, close friends, and immediate family—Bob, Nancy and Jeff, Jeannie and John, Patrick, Destiny, and Nate—are my rock. I love you.

I am also grateful for myriad heroes of faith, mentors (including Dr. George Morris), pastors, and teachers. God uses you in neat ways. Thank you.

God of Joseph, I am in awe of you. How is it that you reveal yourself over and over again to me? I celebrate your presence with Joseph and with me as I study and share. I bless you; I worship you. My hope is that in sharing what you reveal, others will embrace you and find light and life in you! Thank you, Lord. Thank you!

Introducing Joseph ben Jacob

I love the Old Testament. I feel connected to the people there—especially to Joseph.

He was not your ordinary Joe,[1] nor was his father an ordinary man. A little background will help us. Joseph was the son of (ben) Jacob, a deceiver. You remember how Jacob made stew, wore hairy gloves and his brother Esau's clothes, and stole Esau's oldest-son blessing. On the run, Jacob encountered God (think stairway to heaven), the God of promise.

"I will be with you" (Genesis 28:15). God promised presence and completion. God would be with Jacob until all was fulfilled. Jacob's response? *If* God keeps his promise, *then* "I will make the LORD my God" (28:21).

Jacob fathered eleven sons and one daughter while living with his uncle Laban. Joseph was the youngest of those sons, born before Jacob moved his burgeoning family from Paddan-Aram back home to Canaan—the Promised Land. God was with Jacob every step of the journey.

Jacob, through it all, did trust God. He trusted God all the rest of his life. Joseph grew up with the God of promise and presence. He heard the stories and learned God's Word from his father. We'll soon see how well Joseph learned the lesson of God's presence.

---

[1] My grandson and I attended *Joseph*, a production of Sight & Sound Theatres in Lancaster, Pennsylvania several years ago. Their production memorabilia includes a magnet he purchased for his Uncle Joe that simply states, "Not Your Average Joe." Joseph was no ordinary Joe!

As to how my study of Joseph began, where do I start? Joseph's words ring in my heart. "You meant it for evil, but God meant it for good." At least, that's the RAM (Ruth Ann Moore) version of Genesis 50:20, words that impacted me for good from my youth. I suppose Joseph became my hero way back then. How did he forgive so easily? Do I trust God enough to believe that even the awful stuff can become good?

Fast forward to the beginning of the twenty-first century. My first grandson renews my interest in Joseph, particularly in Joseph's integrity. I pray that my Buddy will be a man of integrity, greatly used of God for good. I teach him about Joseph. I take him to a production; I show him Joseph movies. I remind him of Joseph. My grandson deals with the awful, but Joseph reminds me of two things. First, God is with Patrick,[2] and second, God has the power to transform the worst into good—something amazing and wonderful! Patrick adeptly manipulates toys that "transform" from one thing to another. God transforms lives. Still, his life circumstances keep me on my knees and test my trust.

That leaves us wondering how this study actually took shape. Well, Anne Graham Lotz is the one to thank here. The Holy Spirit used her book, *Magnificent Obsession,* to inspire me to study Joseph in a manner similar to the way she studied Abraham. Her manner of writing and the insights God gave her motivated me. I dedicated a year or so to my study, starting in August 2013. My obsession with God through my hero, Joseph, goes on. My family and friends encourage me to share what I learn, and I continue to do so.

---

[2] Patrick gave me permission to share these thoughts.

I admire Joseph for many reasons, most of all because of the God we both trust and depend upon. I share these insights as my prayer that your own encounters with God will be transformative and powerful, for great good!

Here, now, is *Joseph: Not Your Ordinary Joe.*

Sold Genesis 39:1-6

Imagine being sold—and by your own brothers, at that! How traumatic to wait in the pit alone and dread being dragged out later to head for the unknown. Joseph's brothers sold him. Sold him! His own brothers! How could they? Like that, his life changed. He was a slave.

Joseph knew he would be sold again. The Ishmaelites, who bought Joseph from his brothers, were slave traders, after all. He ended up sold to an Egyptian—which was, apparently, an ultrainsult. As if it wasn't bad enough already, the Bible makes a point of emphasizing that Joseph now lived in the house of "the Egyptian."

Joseph, it seems, was sold into the worst-case scenario, not because of the house itself, but because this home was so different than anything he'd ever known. It was going to be hard enough to adjust to being away from home, family, and everything familiar and instead learn a new language, culture, and life of servitude instead of freedom. But on top of that, this wasn't the home of just any ordinary Egyptian family. This Egyptian was powerful and wealthy. This Egyptian had influence with the who's who of Egypt—the wealthy and the influential. There were extra expectations in this Egyptian's home. It wasn't going to be easy adapting to the who's who.

Joseph was a farm boy, more comfortable around sheep than headdresses and elaborate wall art. He knew simplicity. He missed his comfortable and comforting coat of colors. Now, Joseph had to walk like an Egyptian. But it was no joke. This was worse than a teen with no iPhone! He'd been *sold*, rejected, and maybe even forgotten. The trail was cooling. How would his dad ever find him?

Ruth Ann Moore

Did God care? Egypt? Of all places!

Yes, God cared, and the record shows the LORD—I AM God—was with Joseph.

The Lord was with Joseph. More than that, the LORD blessed Joseph "as he served in the home of his Egyptian master" (Genesis 39:2).

Egypt, Egypt, Egypt! What are you doing in your Egypt? Are you wasting your time lamenting your "soldness"—rehearsing how you got there and wallowing in your bitterness about it? Are you caught up in homesickness and immobilized by fear or discomfort? Learn from Joseph.

Joseph served. He actively adapted to Egypt. He learned the language, followed his Egyptian master's instructions and rules, and made the most of his circumstances. Was he always cool, calm, and collected? I doubt it, but the LORD—his God and true master—was with him. Joseph was never alone in Egypt. The one sale that mattered was that his heart was sold on the God of his father and grandfathers.

The I AM God will never leave you or forsake you, even if you're sold and stuck in your own Egypt.

Potiphar: Captain of the Palace Guard

What might it be like to have someone run your affairs so adeptly that the only thing you had to think about was your dinner? You certainly couldn't leave your important matters to just anyone. You would require great trust in that person. We hear too many stories of caretakers stealing from the elderly they supposedly protect. Prisons fill with those who swindle rather than manage the funds of businesses and individuals. Yet, Potiphar's slave, Joseph, was a man of such great integrity that Potiphar had no worries—save his dinner menu, and he could have left that to Joseph, too, if he wanted.

As Pharaoh's officer, Potiphar had influence and wealth. He was used to getting what he wanted, looking good, and living well. With Joseph in charge, Potiphar's household flourished, and Potiphar reaped the benefits. It's no wonder he took a liking to this good-luck charm. He took the Israelite slave under his wing. Potiphar trusted Joseph, until …

Potiphar was older than Joseph. He may have been incapable of having a sexual relationship with his wife—many officials in the service of kings were eunuchs. Scripture is unclear on this. Potiphar did, however, possess the jealousy one might expect when his wife accused Joseph of raping her.

Joseph's good looks made the press. Rarely does Scripture describe physical characteristics, but Joseph was one handsome dude! How did the young Hebrew gain his attractiveness? The LORD was with him (Genesis 39:2, 21, 23).

Did Potiphar forget about Joseph after throwing him in jail? What do you think? Zoom ahead a little to find out. Pharaoh (Potiphar was the captain of his guard) threw his cupbearer and baker into prison—the same one where Joseph hung out now. Guess where the prison was. In the palace of Potiphar!

Potiphar had his eye on Joseph the whole time. Guess what Joseph's new assignment was. Yup, he was in charge of Pharaoh's blacklist employees.

Why do you suppose Potiphar trusted Joseph so much, even in his fury and rage? Potiphar knew he and his household were blessed—even prisoners in his palace dungeon were blessed—because Joseph prospered. Joseph's source of success (and what is success but being useful in whatever circumstances we find ourselves) was his relationship with God. Joseph prospered because he meditated on God. And here's the cool thing about meditating—to meditate actually means "to mumble or speak to yourself" about God.

Do you meditate? Do you do so constantly, speaking to yourself the truth that God is for you? Do you tell yourself how faithful God is, even in the worst of circumstances? Can you have a party even in the emergency room, or can you laugh while tears of loss run down your face? Will you tell yourself that God's steadfast love and mercy are new every morning? Then you, too, will prosper as Joseph. You, too, can be successful, even in jail, and even when you are there under false charges.

Potiphar knew good when he saw it. I wonder if he mumbled and spoke to himself about Joseph's God. I think he did!

Integrity: Joseph and Abimelech Genesis 20

Suppose you are a king, a mayor, or some such person in charge, living day to day and taking care of your people. One day, a stunning woman comes to town. The man she's with says she's his sister.

Suppose your custom is to have a harem of women—the best you can find—at your beck and call.

Suppose something isn't quite right with your libido, and you never get around to sleeping with Sarah. You shake your head about that, until your dream.

"Abimelech, you're a dead man!" That'll get your attention!

Me? Why? What did I do? I'm innocent!

Sarah is another man's wife. "Yes, I know you are innocent," comes the reply. "Your integrity is intact because I protected you," says God.

Think about this for a moment.

Are you a person of integrity, innocent of some unknown sin? How can that be, since we all sin and fall short of God's glory?

I wonder just how often God protects the Abimelech in us before we come to faith in him. This is grace greater than all our sins.

Joseph, like Abimelech, knew temptation. Potiphar's wife was beautiful—maybe not as stunning as Sarah, but attractive in her own right. But Joseph did not sin. He had, like Abimelech, integrity

5

of heart. How? Here, the two men were the same—God protected them. Remember that God was with Joseph.

The difference between Abimelech and Joseph—both men who acted with innocence and integrity regarding beautiful women—was a choice. Joseph chose integrity. Joseph chose to flee from temptation to maintain his faith and faithfulness.

Abimelech might have sinned with Sarah—probably bringing God's wrath on Gerar, since God had already "closed up all the wombs" of his own household because of Sarah (Genesis 20:18)—had God not protected him. Was he afflicted with impotence? Did he have low testosterone? Might he have benefitted from a pharmaceutical product? All we know for sure is that God's protection was effective.

Integrity, Joseph style, is a choice. Choosing the right thing is not always easy. Sometimes we end up in the palace dungeon—alone. Or are we? Even there, God was with Joseph (Genesis 39:23).

So how did it go for Abimelech? Did he die? Let's look at Genesis 20 for answers. Here's what happened:

1. He heeded the warning, right away! (20:8)
2. He told his servants all about it (no secrets), and even they were scared.
3. He got Abraham there on the double—calling him on the carpet for his "sister" ruse (20:9–13).
4. He gave Abraham gifts and protection (to live where he wanted in Gerar) (20:14–16).
5. He and his household were healed when Abraham prayed (20:17–18).

I think Abimelech's integrity *after* his brush with death was much more intentional—maybe even Joseph-like!

Joseph: Integrity in the Face of Temptation

Potiphar's wife knew handsome when she saw it. She wanted Joseph and propositioned him—repeatedly.

Joseph refused her advances—repeatedly. He gives us a model to follow when we face recurring temptation.

- Refuse temptation. Joseph refused immediately (Genesis 39:8). Refusing to entertain wickedness sets the tone for obedience when the tempter keeps at it.
- Recognize that temptation is wickedness. Although many people today downplay the role of sin in temptation, Joseph teaches us that giving in to temptation is wickedness—sin (Genesis 39:9). Keeping ourselves close to God as Joseph did helps us! Before God wrote the commandments on stone tablets and before Joshua called us to meditate daily on the Book of the Law, Joseph stayed grounded in God by relying on his relationship with God.
- Regard relationship. Joseph knew that sexual promiscuity—before or after marriage—is sin. Is your relationship with God so strong that you do all you can to avoid sinning against God? Joseph's was. And Joseph didn't have the advantage of a printed Bible available to him. But we do. The psalmist gives a God-relationship strengthener. "Thy word have I hid in mine heart that I might not sin against God" (Psalm 119:11 KJV). When we memorize Scripture, the Holy Spirit uses that hidden treasure to help our resolve and resistance.
- Remove yourself from temptation whenever possible. Joseph resisted, in part, by staying away from Potiphar's wife. She

didn't give up, but he kept clear of her most of the time. When at last, she had him all to herself—no other men were in the house—she pounced, and Joseph ran!
- Run—literally if necessary. Run away before the tempter can sink the claws of sin into you. The Tempter (the Devil in 1 Peter 5:8) is on the prowl, seeking someone to devour. Run from temptation; leave your shirt behind, if necessary.

Joseph's relationship with God mattered most to him. He prized his faith and faithfulness, refused to dishonor Potiphar, and refused to dishonor God. Joseph's readiness to resist sin revealed his heart. Will you:

- Refuse temptation?
- Recognize sin for what it is—wickedness and evil?
- Regard your relationship with God (and others) as vital, a means to resist sinning?
- Remove yourself, and if necessary,
- Run from temptation?

Your integrity is at stake!

Suffering Joseph

James knew Joseph. He must have. Although he did not name Joseph in his litany on suffering in James 5, he must have had Joseph in mind.

Jail time for Joseph was long. He felt forgotten. Time dragged by. Even though Joseph was the right-hand man to the jailer, he was a prisoner. Dungeons, even those in palaces, are still dungeons—dark, dank, smelly death traps. Prisons are prisons, whether of mind or body.

For more than two years, Joseph rotted in jail—and he hadn't committed a crime! He suffered unjustly. James says, "We give great honor to those who endure suffering" (James 5:11). Job is the obvious sufferer in James' writing; yet Joseph is in the same category.

Joseph, like Job, was patient in his suffering. He diligently took care of the chief jailer's concerns (Genesis 39:23). He woke up and served faithfully day after day. (Can you imagine serving like that in prison?) He slept night after night in the dampness—or did the chill keep him awake? Scripture does not tell us if Joseph got sick or battled dungeon diseases, but his mind and spirit stayed strong. We know this. Genesis 39:23 records the affirmation of the Lord's presence—with him!

Are you in the pits? Do you feel forgotten? What injustice are you suffering? Joseph encourages us to stay faithful and maintain our integrity, even in prison. James says, "From his [Job's, in this verse, but it certainly applies to Joseph, too] experience we see how the Lord's plan finally ended in good, for he is full of tenderness and mercy" (James 5:11).

Suffering is a part of life. Examples dot many pages in Scripture. But here's the deal: in the dark, dank places of our lives, while we feel forgotten—especially when we feel forgotten by God—there is a plan for good. Yes, suffering is awful. Job talked about the nonstop churning inside him (Job 30:27). Yet Job and Joseph both know from experience that God delivers the one who suffers (Job 36:15). The Psalmist confirms this: "My comfort in my suffering is this: Your promise preserves my life" (Psalm 119:50 NIV).

Yes, I think James had Joseph in mind as he wrote to the suffering believers of his day. Persecutions like those they suffered close in on modern believers, too. We can take courage, pray in the face of suffering, and keep on singing praises to God like Job and Joseph (James 5:13) for God has a plan! His plan is for good, and it will come. Stay tuned to Joseph (or reread Job 42:10–17).

Happy in Prison? Yes, Even There!

Here's Joseph again—this time in Psalms. Psalm 119:1–16 tells us that people of integrity (think Joseph) are happy when they follow the law of the LORD. The Josephs are happy because:

- They do not compromise with evil (v. 3).
- They stay pure by obeying and following God's Word and rules (v. 9).
- They memorize God's Word to prevent sin in their lives (v. 11).
- They review God's commandments orally (v. 13).
- They rejoice in God's decrees (v. 14).
- They study the commands (v. 15).
- They delight in God's principles (v. 16).

Aha, so this was how Joseph survived prison.

But, wait a minute, you may say. Joseph was jailed before the commands were given. Yes and no. Moses and the Ten Commandments had yet to enter the biblical record. However, Joseph's great-grandfather talked and walked with God. Abraham had face-to-face encounters with Jesus[3] (Genesis 17:1–14; 18:1–5, 22–33). God made a covenant.

---

[3] Many scholars believe—as I do—that visitations of God in the Old Testament were actually Jesus. Joseph's father, Jacob, saw God face to face and marveled that he lived to tell about it (Genesis 32:30). Exodus 33:20 records God's word to Moses that no one can see God's face and live. Yet Moses spoke face to face with God and even veiled the glory of God on his face. Scripture assures us that Jesus was God in the flesh and as such, revealed God to humans (John 1:18). Jesus made, and makes, God known.

Some of the scholars include Origen; Martin Luther; Jonathan Edwards *Prophecies of the Messiah* in The Works (1835) p. 564; J Douglas MacMillan, author of *Wrestling with God: Lessons from the life of Jacob* (1991) Evangelical Press of Wales,

God called Abraham to obey the covenant. Circumcision was the sign of the covenant instituted by Abraham's obedience—that very day.

Joseph saw the sign of the pact between God and Abraham every day. In his flesh, Joseph was reminded of the meeting between his forefather and God. Joseph recited the command, held it in his heart, and delighted in God's principles—yes, long before stone tablets held the writing of God.

God himself directed Abraham and his sons (including Joseph) to keep the way of the LORD and do what is right and just (Genesis 18:19). So, yes, the imprisoned Joseph was happy. He was happy as a man of integrity who knew, loved, and obeyed God's commands.

Our Joe may have even been happy in an ironic way. His brother Asher's name in Hebrew means blessed (Genesis 30:13). Asher's mother, Leah, was happy to give birth to another son. We hear this blessed happiness as Jesus speaks in Matthew 5:3–12. (Check it out!)

If happiness is missing from your life, you might want to reconnect with Joseph—and the God he served with integrity.

---

and Leonard Sweet and Frank Viola, authors of *Jesus: A Theography* (2012) Thomas Nelson, Nashville.

He's Not Listening

"He's not listening to me," came the cry of a troubled one complaining about God. Don't we sometimes feel that way, too? We ask, "God, do you care? Don't you see what I'm going through?" Did Joseph ask the same questions? I wonder if Joseph thought God had stopped listening.

There are Scripture assurances that God was with Joseph. God is with us. Christmas is the guarantee for believers. The angel said, "They shall call His (Jesus's) name Emmanuel, meaning God is with us," (Matthew 1:23). God is with us. God's "withness"[4] does not mean life is smooth sailing. That presence gives us grace in hard times.

Isaiah "reminds" Joseph—and us—"But as for you, Israel my servant, Jacob my chosen one, descended from my friend Abraham, I have … chosen you and will not throw you away. Don't be afraid, for I am with you. Do not be dismayed, for I am your God. I will strengthen you. I will help you. I will uphold you with my victorious right hand" (Isaiah 41:8–10). Isaiah 43:1–4 shows how very precious you are to God. Joseph was, too.

Joseph was in the pit, hated by his brothers. He was in the dungeon, forgotten by Pharaoh's cupbearer. But God was with him.

Your circumstances may try to convince you that you are abandoned, alone, and forgotten, that God is not listening. Whether you feel God or not, he is with you as he was with Joseph and Israel. No pit is too deep for Emmanuel. No flood can prevent God from being with us. No trouble you face is too overwhelming for God.

---

[4] Sweet PhD, 2012

You may not sense God's presence. You may not hear his voice. You may not see answers to your prayers, but God is with all those who trust and call upon him. "When you go through deep waters and great trouble, I will be with you ... for I am the Lord your God, the Holy one of Israel, your Savior" (Isaiah 43:2–3).

Joseph trusted in his darkest hours. Will you?

Potiphar Calmed Down Genesis 39:19–40:4

Potiphar calmed down. Genesis 39 shows us Potiphar's fury over Joseph's alleged rape attempt. In Genesis 40, Pharaoh was angry, but now Potiphar was level-headed. Pharaoh cast two employees (his cupbearer and baker) into the prison at Potiphar's house. Potiphar knew just the guy to be in charge of the men—Joseph.

Time has a way of calming fury. Time allowed Potiphar to look at Joseph with a clear perspective. Perhaps there was nothing Potiphar could do to release Joseph—at least not yet. Perhaps he wasn't quite convinced of Joseph's innocence—yet. We don't know.

What we do know is this—Potiphar remembered Joseph's work ethic. He recalled the successes in his household when Joseph was in charge. Can we point to Scripture to back up our claim? Indeed, we can (Genesis 39:2–6)! Genesis 40:4 simply says Potiphar assigned Joseph to care for Pharaoh's outcasts.

Potiphar knew Joseph. His rage simmered down enough that he could consider Joseph's character. He knew Joseph was the man for the job.

Potiphar's assignment was focused, not made in the heat of fury. With the passage of time came clear thinking. Maybe by now Potiphar knew Joseph was innocent of his wife's charges. Even if he still believed in Joseph's guilt, he knew integrity when he saw it.

Potiphar chose Joseph for this new job in affirmation of Joseph's positives. What Potiphar had seen and experienced allowed him to trust Joseph—and Joseph's God—even now.

We get angry. We make decisions in our wrath that have long-term consequences. We may not be able to undo those consequences. We can, however, calm down. Once we are able to think clearly, we are challenged to make decisions based on wisdom and truth. Joseph was on the receiving end of both anger-laced actions and clearheaded empowerment.

As for me, I'd like to emulate the calm Potiphar and empower prisoners. Potiphar's choice to put Joseph in charge was the beginning of Joseph's path to freedom. Stay tuned!

Joseph Paid Attention Genesis 40:1-23

Joseph was a detail person. He paid attention. If Joseph were your son or husband, around you daily, what might he notice about you? Genesis 40:6 shines a light on one kind of detail that was important to Joseph: "The next morning Joseph noticed the dejected look on their faces."

Joseph was in Potiphar's dungeon. Pharaoh's chief cupbearer and baker were his cellmates. Scripture details about them are sketchy. What did the bad guys do? Were they really bad, or were they falsely accused like Joseph?

Potiphar entrusted Joseph with the care of the two men. Joseph woke up the morning after they both had dreams—nightmares, by the sound of it. Joseph noticed a dejected look on their faces. Not only did Joseph see worry lines, but he also cared about the cause.

Joseph may have asked, "What were your dreams about? Why did they trouble you so?" The answer of the men strikes me, gives me questions of my own. They were worried because no one was there in the dungeon to interpret their dreams. Does that mean Pharaoh had a dream man on his payroll? Was it common to have a dream interpreter nearby? It turns out that Pharaoh did have access to "magicians and wise men of Egypt" (Genesis 41:8). It sounds to me like our modern swami, Tarot-reading, tea-leaf-studying, fortune-telling types. "Interpreting dreams is God's business," was Joseph's response in Genesis 39:8—God's business alone.

So Joseph saw, and he cared, that his roomies were distressed by their dreams. (If you dream dreams as strange as mine, you'd be puzzled for sure and quite possibly distressed! But back to Egypt.) "Tell me," Joseph invited.

The cupbearer dreamed of a budding fruit vine with three branches that bore rich grapes he squeezed into Pharaoh's cup. Joseph listened, and because God was with him as the interpreter, Joseph knew the meaning. Within three days, the cupbearer would get his job back. Joseph asked that when he was back at work, he remember Joseph. He requested that the cupbearer ask Pharaoh to get him out of there, since he was innocent.

The baker dreamed of three baskets of rich pastries prepared for Pharaoh were on his head, but the birds pecked at them. God revealed the coming doom for the baker. Joseph understood. Did Joseph hesitate to share this meaning? There's no such Scripture indication, but I would not want to tell the baker that Pharaoh would cut off his head in three days and leave his body out for the birds to peck at.

Three days later, it all happened just as Joseph described. Read Genesis 40:1–23 for all the details.

Details matter to God—and to Joseph. The details of your life matter. Do you trust God and pay attention to his wisdom like Joseph? If so, even a dungeon can be a place of blessing and light. If not, what do you need to do today? You don't want to end up like Pharaoh's baker!

"For God so loved the world [that includes you] that he gave his only Son [that's Jesus], so that everyone [including you] who believes in him [Jesus] will not perish [like Pharaoh's baker] but have eternal life. God did not send his Son into the world to condemn it, but to save it" (John 3:16–17).

Joseph and Jesus

Both were shepherds, both greatly loved by their fathers. What do you know about Joseph and Jesus? What might we discover by comparing these heroes of the Christian faith? Joseph and Jesus, it turns out, shared many things. Several good parallel lists exist. The *MacArthur Study Bible* has one of those lists. Another was published by Jews for Jesus in their November 1985 newsletter. My own compilation follows this chapter. The following are but a few of the commonalities.

Both Joseph and Jesus had brothers who hated them. Each of them found themselves in the crosshairs of those who wished them harm. Joseph's brothers took his robe and used it to deceive their father, while soldiers took Jesus' robe and gambled over it (Genesis 37:23, John 19:23–24).

Both heroes traveled to Egypt—though not as a pleasure trip. Joseph had slave years ahead of him, and Jesus lived there as a baby until the murderous Herod was dead. Joseph's brothers sold him for the slave price of twenty pieces of silver. Judas sold Jesus for a slave price as well (Genesis 37:26, Matthew 2:14–15).

Temptation tried hard to reduce these saviors to common sinners—Joseph saw Potiphar's wife and knew what she wanted, but he ran away. Jesus, after forty days of hunger, did not bite at the tempter's offer of bread or power (Genesis 39:7, Matthew 4:1–4)!

Joseph and Jesus were each falsely accused. Chains bound them both (Genesis 39:20, Matthew 27:2). While in custody, each was with two other accused men. Each set of companions included one rescued man and one criminal deserving of his punishment. Both Joseph and

Jesus suffered and were exalted to high positions when their suffering ended (Genesis 41:41, Philippians 2:9–11).

Joseph began his work as Egypt's overseer at age thirty (Genesis 41:46). Jesus was about the same age when he started his public ministry (Luke 3:23).

Scripture memory is easy if you memorize John 11:35: "Jesus wept!" Are you aware that Scripture records Joseph's tears, too? See Genesis 42:24 and Genesis 45 for examples of Joseph weeping.

Joseph and Jesus forgave (Genesis 45:1–15, Luke 23:34). How do we handle the wrongs done against us? Look at Joseph's story to see how he forgave. Remember that Joseph was human, not divine like Jesus. For greater help in forgiveness, call upon Jesus, who can offer you the same spirit and power within him!

Ultimately, Joseph and Jesus were saviors—Joseph of his own nation and Egypt, Jesus of Israel, the world, and all who believe in him for eternity (Genesis 45:7, Matthew 1:21).

Evil happens. Our times prove this truth. But with Joseph[5] (and Jesus), we can declare, "You meant it for evil but God meant it for good to save many lives" (Genesis 50:20).

---

[5] Joseph was reassuring his brothers that God had everything under control, that his years in Egypt had purpose. All of our experiences are opportunities for God to bring good out of bad! Thanks be to God.

Joseph and Jesus Parallels Chart

Joseph and Jesus in Scripture

Joseph	What They Share	Jesus
Genesis 30:1, 22-23	Miraculous birth	Matthew 1:18-25; Luke 1:26-37
Genesis 37:2	Shepherding sheep for his father	John 10:11, 27-29
Genesis 37:3	A father who loves him	Matthew 3:17
Genesis 37:4	Brothers who hate him	John 7:4-5
Genesis 37:20	Physical harm at the hand of others	Hebrews 2:11
Genesis 37:23	A garment lost	John 19:23-24
Genesis 37:26	Time in Egypt	Matthew 2:14-15
Genesis 37:28	Sold for a slave price	Matthew 26: 15
Genesis 39:21-23	Favor with jailer/guard	Matthew 27:54
Genesis 39:7	Tempted	Matthew 4:1
Genesis 39:16-18	False accusations	Matthew 26:59-60
Genesis 39:20	Bound in chains	Matthew 27:2
Genesis 40:1-8, 20-22	Blessed one and judged other fellow prisoner	Luke 23:32
Genesis 39: 2-6	Suffering - though ruler over him knew his true character or suspected innocence	Matthew 27:19-24
Genesis 41:41	Dramatic "resurrection" after suffering	Philippians 2:9-11
Genesis 41:46	Mid-life when ministry began (30 years)	Luke 3:23
Genesis 42:24, 45:2, 14-15, 46:29	Tears	John 11:35
Genesis 45:1-15	Forgiving spirit	Luke 23:34
Genesis 45:3	Revelation of identity to brothers/followers	Acts 1:3; 1 Corinthians 15:5-8
Genesis 45:7	The hope of his nation rested on him	Matthew 1:21
Genesis 50:20	Rested in God's faithfulness despite evilness done to him	Luke 22:42-43, 23:43; John 19:11a

Samaria's Well *John 4*

Why did I never see it before? Jacob gave a well to Joseph. When did that happen and why? Joe was not an ordinary shepherd (like his brothers). Why did he need a well?

Nevertheless, John, the beloved, recorded the location of Joe's well. It was in Samaria. Specifically, the well Jacob passed on to Joseph was in Sychar. Here's what strikes me—this was the very well in the record of Jesus' encounter with "the woman at the well" (John 4:5). Wow! My heart beats within me; my emotions swell so that I can barely record God's amazing work here. Let me explain.

You already know how Joseph ministers to me, how he is my hero. Fully two years after beginning this study of his life, I continue to draw from the deep well of Joseph.

I see Joseph in Job, for example. Job is called a man of integrity—such great integrity that even the loss of children and health could not separate the man from his desire to praise God, no matter how painful. But I digress.

John 4 is one of the New Testament stories I resonate with. I have preached more than one sermon on this Samaritan woman and her encounter with Jesus at the well. She was alone (outcast, really—friendless), out at noon (not your ordinary time to draw water). She was a woman (doomed by her gender, too). And she was divorced! Could things have been any worse for her?

With downcast eyes and slumped shoulders, she dragged herself in the heat of the day to draw the water necessary for the day—day after day, jug after jug in the unwelcome ordinariness of it all.

Jesus, with sweat glistening on his brow and dust coating his feet and sandals, sat at the well—Joseph's well. Waiting for a drink, for someone to come and draw water at noon, was like throwing a snowball in July.

But Jesus was in the perfect place at the perfect time! She came and drank the living water Jesus offers. Like Joseph, this Samaritan woman was in the right place at the right time to receive and then offer new life and hope to her family and village—even those who previously had no time for her!

The well of God's love is deep. The living water becomes a "perpetual spring within" that attracts others to Jesus (John 4:14). Joseph drank from the well, too, and not just because Jacob gave it to him. Joseph drank because of the drink Jesus offered. Then he shared the drink with his brothers.

Will you drink, too? Will you allow Jesus to lift your sagging heart? You drink, and the spring within begins to flow. Joseph drank, and the nation of Israel's sons (and daughters) is alive and well two thousand years later. A Samaritan woman drank, and a whole village listened to Jesus. Just imagine the possibilities!

Who but God could bring Joseph, Jesus, and a Samaritan woman together at one specific well? I am in awe!

Integrity Matters *Genesis 40:20-23*

"Whoever walks in integrity walks securely, but whoever takes crooked paths will be found out" (Proverbs 10:9 NIV).

"Be sure your sin will find you out" (Deuteronomy 32:23 KJV). My kids heard this verse more often than they wanted to as they were growing up. Proverbs 10 puts a more positive spin on the words of Moses.

Integrity gives us sure footing in life. Integrity can see us through dangers and places where our vision is obstructed—think dense fog or thick snow.

Just what is integrity? Honesty, truthfulness, veracity, reliability, honor, and uprightness—these synonyms can be helpful to reveal integrity to us. O. S. Hawkins in *The Joshua Code* defines integrity this way: "Integrity is that state or quality of being complete, and it is freedom from corrupting influences or motives."[6]

"Freedom from corrupting influences" means that even in the midst of stuff, we can stand tall, maintain our honor, be truthful, and walk securely. With integrity, we can be who God created and called us to be. We can be authentic and true—to God and to ourselves.

Corruption is ever with us. Crooked paths abound. The unknown is dangerous and scary. All of this was true in Joseph's life, too. Angry brothers, slave traders, a lying woman, forgetful cellmates—these were Joseph's crooked paths. But he walked in integrity. Joseph's steps were secure and led to his high position in Egypt. Integrity

---

[6] Hawkins, O. S. *The Joshua Code*. Nashville: Thomas Nelson Publishers, 2012. Book.

matters. Just ask the baker whose sin caught up to him. His lack of integrity got him executed. It wasn't pretty (Genesis 40:20–22).

Are you walking in integrity? Are you complete in your relationship with God like Joseph was? Your walk in life needs the sure footing of integrity, complete with honesty before God and truthfulness with others. "Whoever walks in integrity walks securely" (Proverbs 10:9 NIV). May it be for you as it was for Joseph!

Joe's Clothes Genesis 37:1-3

Costumes can be creative and fun with colors, patterns, and intricate designs. When *The Muppet Show* was popular and Kermit and Miss Piggy were childhood heroes, one seamstress graced her grandchildren with costumes of the duo. A lot of work went into the making. Lavish love was stitched into every seam. Jacob, also known as Israel, created a special coat for his beloved Rachael's first son, Joseph.

That coat got Joseph into trouble with his brothers. Why? Let the Word tell you. "Now Israel loved Joseph more than all his children, because he [was] the son of his old age: and he made him a coat of [many] colors" (Genesis 37:3 KJV). Now imagine you are Joseph. You are a teen. You wear what you like, over and over, day after day. You know your dad loves you extravagantly. Your coat has color and pizzazz! Your brothers' clothes? They are drab, earth-toned, and non-distinct. They are clothes that meet the need—but your coat yells, "Favored son!"

Another Father clothed his Son, too. The coat was not like Joseph's. Oh, the Son was favored, for sure, but the Dad had an odd way of showing it. Jesus's coat of human flesh was painful to wear, subject to decay, and resulted in his death. No kingly robe for Jesus, just swaddling clothes and a manger bed for the Son of the Highest. Wait a minute!

Did God not know the favor of Israel for Joseph? Did he not get that the clothes make the man? Oh, he understood, all right. In fact, God was making sure that Jesus's siblings (you and me) would not be jealous of his clothes.

Jesus wore skin—human flesh. This gave Jesus an inside view into humanity. The apostle John said that the Word (who was with God and who was God—Jesus) "became flesh" (John 1:1–14). Paul later said about Jesus that he "made himself of no reputation, and took upon him the form of a servant, and was made in the likeness of men" (Philippians 2:7 KJV).

Joseph's clothes set him apart and made him a target. Irony strikes, because Jesus's clothes did the exact same thing. "[Jesus] grew up before him like a tender shoot, and like a root out of dry ground. He had no beauty or majesty to attract us to him, nothing in his appearance that we should desire him" (Isaiah 53:2 NIV). So what is the common thread between Joseph's clothes and Jesus's? Glory. Lavish love. Love so great that it lays its own life down to save others.

Joseph's robe landed him in a pit that was the entrance to life for his brothers. The human family can be so cruel—just look at Jesus on the cross, his fleshly robe mangled and lifeless. Yet that very cross is our entrance into life and to glory.

Whether you wear colored robes and are blessed with favor or your clothes are drab and perhaps painful, Jesus knows what you are going through. (Remember, he wore our flesh.) The Father God wants to clothe you majestically. Think of the parable of the Prodigal Son. The father ran to greet his repentant son. "The father said to his servants, Bring forth the *best* robe, and put [it] on him; and put a ring on his hand, and shoes on [his] feet" (Luke 15:22 KJV, emphasis mine). The same God who brought good out of Joseph's troubles and raised Jesus from the dead will clothe you with life, if you hang on by faith. Listen to Jesus: "He that overcometh, the same shall be clothed in white raiment; and I will not blot out his name out of the book of life, but I will confess his name before my Father, and before his angels" (Revelation 3:5 KJV).

With Isaiah, we can celebrate: "I will greatly rejoice in the LORD, my soul shall be joyful in my God; for he hath clothed me with the garments of salvation, he hath covered me with the robe of righteousness, as a bridegroom decketh [himself] with ornaments, and as a bride adorneth [herself] with her jewels" (Isaiah 61:10 KJV).

Joe's clothes are all right!

Joe's Clothes, Postscript Genesis 41:37-46a

Joseph's first colorful coat was a gift from his father. The love of a dad, an *abba*, is a gift in itself. Love was woven into that coat. And favoritism. Jacob clearly favored Joseph.

Joseph got another robe from Pharaoh. This one had nothing to do with either love or favoritism—unless you consider God's favor to Joseph.

Here was Joseph, fresh out of jail—maybe two or three hours of freedom, if that. Pharaoh just met Joseph. There was no time even for pleasantries between them; he dressed Joseph in the best Egypt had to offer.

Does that not amaze you? It should. Or maybe it should not. All Pharaoh knew about this Hebrew before him was that his God could interpret dreams. Oh, maybe Potiphar put in a good word for Joseph based on his management of the Potiphar household pre-prison. Truth be told, Pharaoh knew nothing about Joseph, yet he gave Joseph his signet ring, too. It boggles the mind to realize the prestige and power Joseph attained on that jailbreak day!

So Joseph had two precious coats. Why? Pharaoh's coat certainly changed his appearance in a hurry!

I think of Joseph and Jesus. Jesus wore different coats. Swaddled in infancy in the rags of poverty, he wore a fine linen robe that soldiers gambled over as he died. Jesus knew the favoritism of his heavenly and earthly fathers. Love clothed him, too, but did not stop his brothers from selling him to the authorities. Jesus became a slave to sin in the dungeon of death. He broke free—we call it resurrection—to wear the robes of righteousness once more.

In Egypt's robes, Joseph provided food and sustained life for the world (during severe famine). In resurrection robes, Jesus is life, providing more than a meal or seed for the field.

Joseph's coats give us a glimpse into the nature of God, the One who sustained him through it all.

What are you wearing today? If you allow Jesus to dress you, I promise your coat will be better than the finery Joe wore in his best days in Egypt!

From Tested to Teacher

It's hard to believe, but true: some folks really do enjoy taking tests. Most students, however, do not! Joseph's tests were not the pen and paper type, and certainly not done on a computer. It's not likely that Joseph gloried in his testing, but he did relish the presence of his God through it all.

God sent Joseph to Egypt, testing his character through slavery and prison (Psalm 105:17–22). I think I will take classroom tests, even timed ones, over iron collars and foot fetters, thank you very much.

These are interesting things, Joseph's tests. Each test of Joseph's life from age seventeen through thirty had purpose, equipping the Hebrew to lead and save lives. God had a whole nation in mind. Despite the current trend to engineer medicine and education toward individuals, God was on the cutting edge in a different way back in Joseph's day. Therefore, Joseph's tests were critical. Salvation for many was at risk.

God's tests are meant for good, to provide a future and hope, to save many lives. Joseph passed the tests—he aced them! But he didn't celebrate his 4.0 grade point average or go on about his victories. Joseph learned well from the master instructor. He humbly thanked God for teaching him. Then he passed on what he learned.

Psalm 105 tells us that Joseph instructed the Pharaoh's aides. He taught the king's advisors. As the ruler over all the Pharaoh's possessions, as second in command in Egypt, Joseph had to be wise. The best teachers are the experienced. Joseph was good at serving. His first master, Potiphar, knew Joseph to work hard. He trusted Joseph's instincts. Prison time gave Joseph the opportunity to learn more, even from the Pharaoh's inside men—the chief baker and chief cupbearer. When the time was just right, Joseph moved out of the testing phase and into his dream job. Hope blossomed for Joseph's father and family because Joseph passed his tests.

Are you in a testing time? Is the wrong going "wronger" and the dark getting darker? Learn from Joseph. Stay faithful to God. God is with you! The tests you take now are meant to bring hope and ultimately save lives. Psalm 105 shows how God delights in deliverance: "So he brought his people out of Egypt with joy, his chosen ones with rejoicing. He gave his people the lands of pagan nations, and they harvested crops that others had planted. All this happened so they would follow his decrees and obey his instructions. Praise the Lord!" (Psalm 105:43–45)

Joseph trusted his teacher—his God—through all his testing. Joseph went on to be a good teacher who made a difference. You can, too!

All Things

It can be hard to see in the moment, especially when the moment is tough or unexpected. Sometimes the revelation only comes in the passage of time. But those who love God do discover that all things work together for good (Romans 8:28). More specifically, God works them together for good. (What an amazing God! Who but he can make even the crummy, unexpected things work for good? How great is his power!) Joseph discovered this, too.

Not just some things work for good—everything, period. Author Robert J. Morgan in his book, *The Promise: God Works All Things Together for Your Good*,[7] states emphatically, "All means all."

Joseph loved the God of his father, his grandfather, and his great-grandfather. Joseph's God was the God of Abraham, Isaac, and Jacob. Abraham believed God, and his belief began a heritage of faith in his family. Abraham believed God could raise up Isaac from the dead. His faith became a reality when God provided a ram to sacrifice (Genesis 22). Isaac remembered this encounter with God. He told his son, Jacob, of his experience. Jacob's personal encounters with God formed the foundation of his faith in and love of the God of his fathers. Joseph grew up hearing the stories of God—how Sarah laughed to think God would really give a son to Abraham in his old age (Genesis 18:12) and how his grandfather was born to 100-year-old Abraham. (Sarah was ninety [Genesis 21:1–6].)

Joseph also knew about the struggles of the faith of his fathers. Abraham left his own father to follow God to the Promised Land,

---

[7] (Morgan, 2010)

but only with struggle. Ishmael caused long-lasting heartache—this son of Abraham's choice to act rather than wait on God for the son of Promise. Joseph's dad, Jacob, was a deceiver and suffered the consequences. Joseph's grandfather on his mother's side, Laban, gave Jacob a run for his money—literally! Jacob ran with two wives, two concubines, and eleven sons, complete with flocks and servants. (Imagine that flight! See Genesis 31:1–18 for details.) Yet during that run, Jacob encountered and fell in love with God. So, Joseph knew that all things meant *all* things.

And we know, too—at least, we can know. When we remember, as Joseph must have done during the struggles of his own life, how our faith in God began, we know that God turns evil into good, that God transforms the struggles. Look into your past. How have struggles, disappointments, loneliness, and other difficulties been transformed? How has God worked good out of bad in your life? You can know that God has worked in good ways on your behalf, whether you recognize it now or not. Ask Him for eyes to see it (much like Elisha's servant in 2 Kings 6:17).

Ask yourself, "Do I love God?" It is in the loving that we see how God brings good out of even the evil things that happen. Joseph loved God. That love, that trust, equipped Joseph to look beyond pain and see God at work, how the hardships of his past were stepping stones, and how God transformed his sorrows into successes that reached far beyond his own family.

It is time to start loving God! It is time to remember the past and create a new future filled with life and hope. Allow Joseph to get you started or pick you up for your new beginning. He spoke the same idea that Paul expressed in Romans 8:28, but coming from Joseph's lips, it sounded this way: "You intended to harm me, but

God intended it for good to accomplish what is now being done, the saving of many lives" (Genesis 50:20 NIV).

"And we know that *all things* work together for good to them that love God, to them who are the called according to his purpose" (Romans 8:28 KJV, emphasis mine).

Blessing Your Family

The story of Joseph steps aside temporarily, inviting King David to share what was on his heart. What was important to David? The chronicler shared David's story in 1 Chronicles 15–16.

The day's celebration was over the top! David's joy was unbridled. The Ark of the Lord was safely in the City of David, no longer resting on the threshing floor of Obed-edom.

David moved the Ark God's way with the Levites carrying it between them, poles across their shoulders, just as God planned. Musicians and priests joined the happy procession. David danced his way into Jerusalem. Worship, praise, thanksgiving, sacrificing, and more marked this joyous day.

Ever the composer of songs of thanks and praise, David gave a new song to Asaph and the Israelites—a song to be sung for generations to come. "Give thanks to the Lord," David sang. "He always stands by his covenant—the commitment he made to a thousand generations. This is the covenant he made with Abraham and the oath he swore to Isaac. He confirmed it to Jacob as a decree, to the people of Israel as a never-ending treaty: 'I will give you the land of Canaan as your special possession'" (1 Chronicles 16:15–18).

David celebrated because of God's faithfulness to Joseph and his family. The same God who was with Joseph through it all is this day (in David's day of celebration, and today, with us) present and worthy of praise!

All Israel celebrated. David gave gifts of food to every man and woman in his kingdom this day. David even prepared for the following day; he set up regular ministering and sacrificing, choosing those (by name!) who would offer thanks to God in the coming days. The celebration was a special one and would be remembered for generations to come.

God blessed Abraham's family with generations of God's faithfulness. That's what David's celebration was all about.

And what did David do at the end of this strenuous day? David blessed his family. First Chronicles 16:43 shares the end of David's day with us: "Then all the people returned to their homes, and David returned home to bless his family."

If you are like me, you might be more likely to go home from this day and hit the sofa or take a nap in your recliner. Some of us might be so exhausted that we snap at our families rather than blessing them. David shows us a better way.

His dancing in 1 Chronicles 15:29 disgusted David's wife, Michal. She stayed home during the celebrating; yet he blessed her. He could have tried to convince her how awesome God is. He might have given her a detailed description of the day's events from his perspective. But he loved her. David blessed her. The blessing is significant. Blessing is something we all need, and we need to bless our families.

David's blessing reminds us of God's promise to Abraham: "I will bless you ... and I will make you a blessing to others" (Genesis 12:2–3). We, too, are blessed to be blessings. Joseph's father, Jacob, pleaded with God for a blessing. He held on during the all-night wrestling match until God blessed him (Genesis 32:26–29). When later introduced to Egypt's king, Jacob blessed Pharaoh (Genesis 47:7). Blessing is the right thing to do.

Blessing holds the power to break down barriers. We don't know how Michal responded to her husband's kindness. Yet we do know that blessing comes from the heart of God, and David is described as a man after God's own heart. The blessing one frequently humbles himself and exalts the blessed one. What might blessing do for our families? What power for good might God unleash as we bless them "and do not curse" (Romans 12:14 NIV)? Let's take David's lead, even at the end of a long and tiring day (no matter how good it may be), and go home to offer blessing to those we love the most!

The Hand of God

The hand of God on the man of God moves mountains for the plan of God.

A man, like Ezra or Joseph—or any other ordinary man, woman, boy, or girl—can be a mountain mover when the hand of God is upon him or her. We see this throughout Scripture, from Genesis to Revelation.

For example, say you wanted to travel from Johnstown, Pennsylvania to Boston, Massachusetts and back. What is the shortest timeframe possible? When the hand of God is upon you, and when a college student needs to be home for her Gram's funeral, you can make that thousand-mile round trek in fewer than twenty-four hours. Say you wanted to get from Babylon, post-exile, and return to Jerusalem to reignite worship in the city of God. How long might that journey take? Hint: no interstate roads existed, at least not roads that allowed for sixty-five-mile-per-hour travel. Ezra's journey took him months. He left Babylon on April 8, 458 BC and arrived in Jerusalem on August 4, 458 BC—four months, to be exact (Ezra 7:1–10).

Ezra's hardships—travel time was but one of them—remind us of Joseph's years-long incarceration on the road to becoming Egypt's Prime Minister, the position of power that accomplished the plan of God to save the lives of his people and many Egyptians, too. Ezra fit into the plan of God differently.

Ezra was a scholar. He loved to study. He particularly loved to study the law of the Lord. Ezra's uncle Moses (with a long line of greats in between the two) carried the tablets down the mountain after the hand of God inscribed them on rock—talk about needing a good book bag! The hand of God on Moses literally moved the mountain—at least a slab or two of rock big enough to hold the law. The plan of God in Ezra's day was about the same as in uncle Moses's day: teach the people the laws and regulations. (The purpose of the law, then and now, is to protect and preserve life!) God wants the people of God to live well!

So Ezra studied and obeyed God's law. No wonder the hand of God was upon him. Joseph determined to obey God, too—and Joseph's resolve came before the law was given to Moses! What about now? Is that powerful hand of God still involved in the lives of the likes of you and me? Does God still see us through the mountains of grief, bullying, financial reversal, or daily drudgery to accomplish God-sized plans?

Do you think, *I'm no Joseph, no Ezra*? Well, good then—God needs you to accomplish his plan for saving lives today! You can obey God's law and determine to obey his commands. God's hand will empower you to make a difference. Thank God for Joseph and Ezra. Learn from their lives and examples of faith, but be yourself. Allow God to move mountains through you in unique and wonderful ways for the accomplishing of his plan!

God's hand on you will enable you to carry out God's plan! Now pick up a rock or two, and start moving that mountain with God.

Experiencing God Pharaoh Style Genesis 41

Two dreams changed everything—for Pharaoh, the Egyptians he ruled, and Joseph.

Pharaoh experienced God in his strange dreams. Fat cows eaten by skinny cows? A full head of grain decimated by a withered one? Joseph understood. He had his own unusual dreams—a lifetime ago when he was a carefree teen. At thirty, with too many years of experience on the hard side of life, Joseph realized that God reveals himself, especially when he is about to accomplish something amazing. God initiates contact, even with a king who considers himself god—as many Pharaohs did.

God revealed what was about to happen. Pharaoh's dreams showed him how it would happen. Seven good crop years would be followed by seven years of famine. You can be sure that when God shows you the what and the how, it will happen. Joseph was so secure in his relationship with God, his confidence in the God of his father Jacob and grandfather Abraham, that he could tell Pharaoh boldly—even barely an hour after his own prison rescue. God set a world of change in motion:

- Joseph's release on the heels of Pharaoh's dreams,
- Egypt's readiness for coming famine (with Joseph's provision plan, they had enough, plus some to spare),
- salvation and reunion for Joseph's own family,
- the birth of a Savior through the lineage of Joseph's brother, Judah (the one who suggested making a slave profit out of Joseph instead of killing the boy [Genesis 37:26–28]), and

- salvation and forgiveness for you and me through the birth of that Savior, Jesus. (See Matthew 1 and Luke 3 for the Jesus-Judah connection.)

Oh, yes! God takes the initiative so we can experience him! Maybe we experience no Pharaoh-like dreams or Joseph-style twists and turns; nonetheless, God shows us his plans for good—yes, even famine was a tool for good in God's plan. And our various challenges, trials, and tests, in God's hands, become opportunities for God to shine—or as Joseph would say, "to save many lives!" (Genesis 50:20)

Where is God inviting you to experience new life today? If you need a Joseph to help you see and understand, God has that person ready to help you. Remember, Joseph started anew after a quick shower and shave. (Clean-shaven was the only way to approach Pharaoh [Genesis 41:14].) God just may have a Joseph ready to shave you, too, so your new life can begin now.

An Overnight Success Genesis 41:1-14

Early one Egyptian morning, Joseph rose, like cream, to the top. An overnight success! If anyone had a rags to riches story to tell, it was Joseph. No bragging on his part, no Facebook posts to like here, but a success like his was remarkable. How do we account for this achievement?

"Reverence for the Lord is the foundation of true wisdom. The rewards of wisdom come to all who obey him," (Psalm 111:10). Wisdom was Joseph's key to success, wisdom birthed in his awe of God even in the dungeon. God blessed Joseph with an understanding of Pharaoh's dreams and insight into how Egypt could survive the coming famine. Joseph thrived on wisdom while a servant to Potiphar, while serving the captain of the guard in the palace dungeon, and then on this amazing morning!

Imagine yourself in such a morning transition. One minute, you hear the screams of tortured prisoners down the hall; the next, you smell Pharaoh's cologne as he tells you his dream. That lifetime-ago minute seems like a dream, but you know it was all too real. This, this gold-necklaced moment, is too much to fathom—that is, if you were trying to make sense of it.

Joseph focused on the dream, on instructing Pharaoh to hear the voice of God through his dream. The God who was with Joseph—Emmanuel—through his darkest days would also be with Egypt in theirs. God's witness even extends to those in the company of God-lovers. And God is with us, with all who love him as Joseph did. So night turned to day for our hero—only his overnight success was thirteen years in the making.

Pharaoh knew extraordinary wisdom when he saw it. Joseph recommended that a key person oversee the collection of grains during years of abundance to prepare for the years of famine. Pharaoh loved Joseph's plan for famine survival. He was so taken with the plan that he put Joseph in that key role. Second in command. Prime Minister. Call it what you will; Joseph's nametag no longer read, "Prisoner." Joseph had a parade to attend, and he was the star attraction.

Joseph's plan worked, and barns were bursting with grains before the famine began. Within seven years—post-prison—Joseph was a daddy to two boys who helped him forget the years of his troubled past and remember the God who made him fruitful in wisdom.

God is with us in our darkest days, however hard we may find that to believe! We may not have a dramatic, overnight success story to tell (or awaiting us), but we can be very sure that the God who was with Joseph is with us. We can be certain that God knows our darkness and is providing a bright dawn for us. We can know with confidence that God's plan for success will blow our socks off, and the wake of success will extend farther than we can imagine. Bottom line? Joseph's God, in whom Pharaoh learned to trust, is worthy of our trust, too. He is the God of success, the God who grants wisdom birthed in our darkest hours.

Journey Markers

I wonder: did Joseph ever see Jacob's journey marker, the one he named Bethel? If I had been Joseph, I would have wanted to see it. This stone marked the spot of his father's dream meeting with God. Dreams seemed to be the thread of God-incidences[8] in Joseph's life.

Jacob's dream became the subject of songs ("Jacob's Ladder"), art, and stories. Jacob dreamed of a stairway to heaven. Jacob encountered God, seeing the God of Abraham and Isaac, his own father, on the top step. To mark the place, Jacob set upright the stone he had used for a pillow. He named the place Bethel—house of God. For Jacob, this place was the gateway to heaven. It was here he learned that God was personal, that God cared about him—and about fulfilling promises made to his fathers.

Joseph heard the story. Just as Jacob heard the stories of Abraham and Isaac and all that God had done for them, Jacob shared his stories with his sons. Our children need to hear our stories of faith, too, of God's promises kept and provisions made. Knowing Joseph's spirit, I know he would have relished seeing the place of Jacob's encounter with God. Journey markers matter.

Meditating on Jacob's marker of faith made me wonder. What are my faith markers? Where are they? What do they mean for my continuing journey in Christ Jesus? I made a neat discovery. My markers reveal changes in me.

---

[8] A friend in ministry, Joseph "Bud" Walls, frequently speaks of God's actions in all the circumstances of life. Bud credits his use of "God-incidence" to a spiritual mentor of ours, the late Jay Brendlinger. He and I concur. There are no coincidences, only "God-incidences."

- There was the time—although no specific place comes with the memory—I asked Jesus to teach me to pray. That request led me into new territory of prayer, still vast and open to exploration.
- A streetlight with its amber glow marked the end of a drought. God's silence persisted for months. He did not answer prayer. He didn't even seem to hear it. What was happening? Was I wrong in praying? Did God care? I remember the walk that evening, the tears. I remember being beneath that streetlight when the assurance came. God was with me. God did hear my prayers. God would never leave me or forsake me. This personal affirmation soothed my soul, and I revisit that streetlight from time to time. I am comforted.
- Not a voice, but a deep inner knowing called me to a specific prayer opening. So scared to step out, to walk into that opening, I lay on my couch, physically ill. My sofa is not the marker. I got up; I went anyway. I prayed in that place. The blue carpet there is my prayer marker. I saw that carpet as I prayed, repeatedly, in that place.

The examination of these stones of my own helps me see where God has led me. Surely, Jacob's marker did that for him, too. Jacob faithfully repeated his stories of faith. Faith passes from one generation to another in the telling of stories. It is time for me to share my markers with my children and grandchildren. I dream of the day my descendants, to the thousandth generation, will know God and be with him forever. A glimpse of my future includes more prayer, more stories. Thank you, Jacob, for putting up your pillow stone!

What are your markers?

Delight

Delight comes in many forms, especially around Christmas time. Delight is joy—the giving or receiving of joy. We see delight in the eyes of children. We enjoy giving good gifts to others. We are joyful in renewed relationships. But did you ever think about the delight that comes in obedience? Do you enjoy obeying commands, especially the commands of God?

Isaiah 11:3 says our Savior, the stump of Jesse's line (a prophetic way of saying Jesus Christ), "will delight in obeying the Lord." I have not always enjoyed obedience.

There was the time Mom sent me with sweeper (for those who live outside the confines of Pittsburghese, this means a vacuum) in hand. "Go do the steps." It was only years later that I discovered she had heard all the grumbling and complaining I thought the sweeper noise swallowed up. There was no delight in that time of obedience! I wonder what kind of job I did in my dour state. All too often, we obey God this same way. And I doubt that the youthful yuk pleases God any more than it pleased my mother.

Joseph clearly took pleasure in obedience. His ability to rise to prominence in Egypt reflected his satisfaction in staying faithful to God, despite any number of opportunities to grumble and complain along the way. Joseph basked in the limelight precisely because his happiness came through compliance with God's directions.

What is God saying to you? Did you obey yet? If you think no one hears your grumbling, think again. There's no noise loud enough to drown out your complaints. Mom still loves me though I railed against her that day. God still loves you, despite your harshest complaints about him. Today is a good day to begin to delight in obedience.

Pay attention to the delights around you. Seek to obey with appreciation and gladness. Determine to please God as young children long to please those they love. This delight in obedience will make God happy. More than that, your obedience will be winsome to others, with the power to draw someone to Christ. Now, that's delightful!

Christmas with Joseph

Mary's husband gets little press, even at Christmas. He's not even our subject today—or is he? You decide. The colored-coat Joseph we've been following had nearly forty generations between him and Jesus, and then he was only an uncle. Jesus descended, on both his mother Mary and his earthly father Joseph's sides, from Judah, brother of our Joseph. A question running through my head today makes me wonder: what would Christmas be like if our Joseph had been in Bethlehem when Jesus was born?

Joseph the carpenter, meet Uncle Joe, the dreamer. Mary had Elizabeth to comfort and confirm her in the pregnancy. Whom did Joseph have? Who would understand the conflicted feelings, yet be certain that this dream was a God thing? Uncle Joe had dream experience; he would have been just the man! As it was, neither the carpenter nor the dreamer was an ordinary Joe, but both held on to their deep faith in God despite odd and trying circumstances in their lives. How does a man work so closely with God (wow—work with God!) and remain humble and graceful at the same time? Perhaps the carpenter looked to the dreamer for solace and strength. He had heard Uncle Joe's story. Tradition dictated its repetition for all children. The carpenter would acquaint his new son with the story, too.

Think of it—baby Jesus in the dreamer's arms. Joseph the dreamer loved being a dad. He held his own sons tenderly, kissed their baby cheeks, and thanked God for their precious lives. He valued the connection—immediate and deep—between babies and their creator. Surely, he would have sensed the oneness between baby Jesus and God. (A name as common then as Bob is nowadays seems an odd choice for the King of kings, but I digress.) Yet God added[9] life through the Christmas child.

God blessed Jacob and Rachel with deep spiritual richness when their Joseph was born. Jacob even gained new life through the son of his old age. (Joseph's management sustained life in Egypt during years of famine.) What did God add to the carpenter's life in this child who was not even his biological son? Apparently not length of years. Joseph only appears in Jesus's story until the boy reached twelve or so. Did God bless the carpenter, or did the Christ child only make his life more—well, Joseph-like? Taking in a pregnant girl, dealing with the town gossip, hustling off to Egypt in a hurry, fearing for the life of the baby boy. What did Mary's husband get out of all of it? If God was adding to his life, it certainly didn't seem to be blessing—was it?

Uncle Joe would understand. The dungeon years looked like anything but blessing. Yet in that dungeon, and in the hardest times of his life, Uncle Joe relied on God's witness to keep him faithful, to make him fruitful and effective. Yes, I believe Uncle Joe did come to Christmas in Bethlehem to add to his nephew's faith.

Joseph, the stepdad of Jesus, shouldered a great burden fathering the God-child his wife bore that first Christmas. His Uncle Joe helped keep him grounded. And God did add—he added life, in the moment and for eternity, to the carpenter in Jesus, the infant he raised to be God's man in the flesh. Hallelujah!

---

[9] The name Joseph means "God adds" or "God has added" (a done deal) in both Hebrew and Greek.

Recipe for Prayer

Ingredients:

Psalm 3—David
Genesis 41—Joseph
Romans 8:1–6—Me

So I woke up this morning, Saturday, January 4, 2014, with a surety that I would pray—but what and for whom I did not know. I began with my daily Psalm; the day's psalm happened to show David being chased by his bad-boy son Absalom. David's confidence in God is amazing. Did David fret? No way! He lay down to sleep, confident in God's victory, no matter what he saw. Yes, I add a generous dollop of David to prayers, especially for those whose circumstances press in upon them. God, grant them a David-like trust that hopes for the best.

And what about Joseph? Was his trail too cold to pick up? Did David get some of his confidence in God through Joseph? I return to Genesis 41:16–36. I find Joseph with Pharaoh, expressing his own certainty in his God. Dream interpretation is God's business, Joseph said, but be ready. Get your planner in place; move ahead with building barns. Joseph trusted God's word so implicitly that he was ready to take action on the spot. Okay, so Joseph's faith and readiness to respond to God are admirable. How did Joseph minister to David? And how do I pray like Joseph?

David grew up with the stories of Abraham, Isaac, and Jacob (Joseph's dad). I can see David mulling over Joseph using his get out of jail free card. Joseph trusted God, even in the bleakest of times. He expected God to act, to be God, no matter what. Joseph waited, but he did not hesitate when the opportunity to act presented itself. I see David modeling the faith he found in Joseph. Listen to David: "But you, O Lord, are a shield around me; you are my glory, the one who holds my head high. I lay down and slept, yet I woke up in safety, for the Lord was watching over me. Victory comes from you, O Lord. May you bless your people."

Joseph's prayers are missing from the Genesis account of his experiences. We know Joseph's pain in prayer from the names of his two sons, born before the end of the famine in Egypt. Manasseh came first. Manasseh helped Joseph forget his hardship. (The name means "God helps me forget" [Genesis 41:51].) We all have things we need to forget in order to move forward, in order to experience God's victories. (Manasseh also helped Joseph forget the pain his family caused him so that he could forgive them and invite them to live with him in Egypt.) Joseph teaches us to pray for divine forgetfulness that readies us to experience redemption. Joseph's second son, Ephraim, shows us the longing of Joseph's heart to be fruitful. Ephraim means "fruitful in the land of my grief" (Genesis 41:52). We, too, experience grief and heaviness of heart; yet we can be fruitful like Joseph and David. My prayer is just this for you and for me. Let's rise above the hurts and sorrows of life. It is our choice.

And this is where Romans 8 enters the mix of our prayer recipe. Because of Jesus, there is no condemnation for those who choose life, who choose to walk and live like Joseph and David, according to the Spirit of life. In my quest to memorize this chapter, I have reached verse 6.[10] Romans 8:6 (NRSV) is clear: "To set the mind on the flesh

---

[10] From my earliest memories, Scripture memorization was important in my family. Matthew 6:33 (KJV) is one of the first verses I learned by heart. "Seek ye first the kingdom of God, and all these things shall be added unto you." The psalmist challenges us to hide God's Word in our hearts that we "might not sin against" God (Psalm 119:11). But a whole chapter? Could I do it in my sixties? My sister memorizes whole books, so I challenged myself to begin with a chapter, and God led me to Romans 8. I invite you to hide God's Word in your heart,

is death, but to set the mind on the Spirit is life and peace." Joseph and David chose to set their minds on the Spirit, on life. God met them and exceeded their expectations of life and peace. God will do the same for you and me if we set our minds on Jesus, on the Spirit who gives us life and peace. My prayer for you—right now, no matter what day or time you are reading this—is that you will choose life.

May you choose to set your mind on the positives that only God can bring, on the potential for good and blessings. May you choose life over death. My recipe for prayer is repeatable. The Spirit led me to examine David and Joseph—and myself. Your ingredients may be others in the Scriptures, but the key to answered prayer is in the Lord of life. In Jesus Christ, the Spirit of life, we find life. May you choose to set your mind on the Spirit today! I am praying for you.

---

too. The rewards are never-ending. Start with something simple. Ask the Lord to show you where to begin.

Seventh Heaven

Joseph must have felt as if he were in seventh heaven during Egypt's years of plenty. Out of jail, Egypt's governor,[11] married. How many times did Joseph pinch himself? How often did Joseph ask God if this was just a dream? The turn of events in Joseph's life was that dramatic.

When we think of life changing in an instant, we often think the reverse. We think of how different life becomes when a loved one dies unexpectedly, or when an accident takes away mobility, for example. On the other hand, Joseph went from rags to riches—literally. Was he dreaming?

We've seen dreams in Joseph's life. Interpreting Pharaoh's dreams about years of plenty followed by years of famine brought Joseph to this place of transformation. But dreaming about change—especially positive change—and actually experiencing life alteration are two different things. Here, Joseph lived his dreams. I wonder if Joseph could have ever anticipated such a dramatic change.[12]

Egypt produced abundant crops, and Joseph collected grain—one fifth of each year's growth amassed so much grain that "granaries were filled to overflowing" after seven years; the grain was like sand on the seashore in its abundance (Genesis 41:49). However, Joseph's personal prosperity, perhaps his greatest blessing, was in the growth of his family.

---

[11] "Since Joseph was governor of all Egypt" (Genesis 42:6).
[12] The possibility of such change is not limited to Joseph: you and I, too, can experience the power of the God "who is able to do immeasurably more than we could ask or imagine" (Ephesians 3:20 NIV). Isn't it amazingly wonderful?

Pharaoh gave the daughter of a priest (that raises questions of its own) to Joseph as a wife. Why the daughter of a priest? Was Pharaoh's intent to cause Joseph to worship the Egyptian gods? Or was it possible that Pharaoh was so struck by Joseph's devotion to God, the awesome God who enabled Joseph to understand Pharaoh's dreams, that he recognized that only a deeply spiritual wife would suit Joseph? I choose to believe that the Holy Spirit was directing Pharaoh in the choice of Potiphera's (an Egyptian priest) daughter for Joseph's new wife, whatever Pharaoh's intentions might have been. They were good together, Joseph and Asenath, and before the seven years of plenty ended, they bore two sons.

Manasseh and Ephraim made Joseph forget his pain and suffering and allowed him to enjoy fruitfulness in Egypt. Did Joseph know that God had once commanded his father Jacob to "be fruitful and multiply"? See Genesis 35:9–15 for the encounter with God that was both life- and name-changing for Joseph's dad. Joseph did know joy. He knew the blessedness of reaping a harvest of plenty. He knew, in tangible ways, that God was with him. And he knew that God was the source of all his blessedness.

We see Joseph in a joyful place. We see God's gifts multiply in Joseph's life. There were blessings ahead for Rachel and her family: "And she conceived, and bare a son; and said, God hath taken away my reproach: And she called his name Joseph;[13] and said, The LORD shall add to me another son" (Genesis 30:23–24 KJV).

God did add another son to Rachel, as she wanted. Although his mother died in childbirth, Joseph loved his younger brother, Benjamin. God added blessings to Joseph through this youngest of the sons of Jacob. And God multiplied Joseph's ability to be a

---

[13] Joseph means "Jehovah has added." Blue Letter Bible http://www.blueletterbible.org/lang/lexicon/lexicon.cfm?Strongs=H3130&t=KJV

blessing even as he blessed Joseph in the reunion with Benjamin that lay ahead.

What are some lessons for us in Joseph's dramatic change?

- God knows where we are at all times—the One who was with Joseph in the dungeon had the razor and clean clothes ready for his meeting with Pharaoh.
- God has prosperity and blessing in store for all who trust in him. Jeremiah 29:11 was as true for Joseph as it is today.
- The good God has planned for us far outweighs the pain and misery of today because all things work together for good for those who love God and are called (like Joseph) according to his purpose (Romans 8:28).
- Joseph's transformation included his mother's dreams and joys—someone has great hopes and dreams for your life, too.
- Your rags to riches story is in the works!

Go to Joseph

I wonder if Pharaoh gave Joseph more than a ring, a fine linen robe, and a gold necklace (Genesis 41:41–42). Genesis 41:55 sounds a little like Joseph got the "The Buck Stops Here"[14] sign, too. The people came to Pharaoh when they were hungry. He referred them to Joseph. "It's his call," Pharaoh told the people. "Do what Joseph says."

Egypt had plenty of grain (Genesis 41:53). Joseph's careful management during the seven years of abundance meant storehouses were full and overflowing. Even surrounding nations knew about Egypt's food supply (Genesis 41:57). Joseph's success showed. However, with the famine underway, personal stores of food did not last long, and the Egyptians became hungry—famished (Genesis 41:55)—with a voracious hunger.[15]

We might say we are famished after a day of playing ball or water-skiing. We come home from a long, busy day at work feeling "starved." The thing is, a table of plenty awaits. And many Americans have stocked freezers and pantries as well. Joseph's contemporaries (both Egyptian and those in surrounding countries), however, had used up their personal supplies. Hunger began to affect them—they were beginning to starve.

---

[14] President Harry S. Truman was famous for having this sign on his desk in the Oval Office, signifying that he wasn't going to abdicate his own responsibility and "pass the buck" on to others, but he was going to both make the decisions that needed to be made and accept the responsibility for his decisions.

[15] As my editor notes, that Egypt had plenty and famished people at the same time seems incongruous. Yet God often gets our attention best when we come to the end of personal resources. God's plenty is available at all times; yet we try to get by on our own. May we hunger for God's plenty and go to Jesus!

A hungry mob can wreak havoc on a government. Maybe Pharaoh was afraid of rebellion, perhaps he was merely shifting the responsibility, or maybe the famine-induced fear caused him to forget that Joseph's God had a plan. Whatever his motives, Pharaoh's answer was directed by God himself. "Go to Joseph," Pharaoh ordered. It was Joseph's hour—time to put his preparations to the test.

Egypt's savior, Joseph, is a picture of God. God's storehouse is running over. He is more than ready to help. God waits until we come to the end of ourselves so we will accept his help. Pharaoh directed his people to seek God's (Joseph's) help in the crisis. Seek God (Joseph), and do what he says. God is able to meet our needs and then some. Will we go? Will we obey?

Why is it that when trouble strikes, we so often try to get through on our own? Even though abundant resources exist, we resist reaching out for help—until we are starving. Then, finally, we cry out, and Pharaoh directs his people and us: go to God. Do what he says.

When there's nothing left, no other resource available, and you are starving, where do you turn? I wonder why it is that we humans so frequently need to come to the end of ourselves, to reach the nothing-left stage before we seek help. The trouble is that we starve ourselves in our quest for self-sufficiency. God stands back and lets us have our way, and we begin to be famished. Oh, we may have plenty to eat all right, but not the right nutrients. A starving child may have more than enough rice but no protein. Pictures of swollen-bellied children are painful reminders of deadly imbalance. If we could see the pictures of ourselves in our spiritual imbalances, we would be just as pained—perhaps more so, for we starve the soul rather than the body.

The good news is that there is escape from famine! We don't need to die, cut off from the plenty of God's eternal storehouses. Egypt's king gave wise advice to all of us. Go to Joseph. Go to God!

Don't Just Stand There!

Fear paralyzes. Famine decimates. People die.

Joseph's brothers had families. Most of the brothers were already grandfathers when the famine hit. Judah's wife and two sons were dead, but his younger sons, Perez and Zerah needed food—and Perez already had two sons of his own. Eleven of Jacob's sons and their families gathered due to the famine. Sixty-six (not counting the wives) members of Jacob's family, paralyzed by fear of starvation, stood, not knowing what to do. To do nothing was certain death for Abraham's descendants. But what could they do?

The survival of Jacob's family weighed heavily on him. Benjamin, his youngest, already had ten sons of his own, and all of them were beyond hungry. As far as Jacob knew, Joseph was dead. He couldn't bear to lose any more—not to famine. So Jacob took charge.

Jacob took his boys aside. His words were direct. In today's vernacular, Jacob admonished his sons, saying, "Don't just stand there!" (The Hebrew question is something like, "Why are you looking at each other?")[16] I've been in situations where I had no clue what to do. Haven't you? I have a sense of the helplessness Joseph's brothers felt as they looked around at one another. "Oh, sure, Dad says, 'Do something'? But what? We can't make the earth produce the crops we need."

Even without television news, Google searches, or Twitter posts, Jacob knew about the food available in Egypt. Going to a foreign country for corn went against the grain of this God-fearing family,

---

[16] The Hebrew verb *ra'ah* here means "to look reflexively, as upon yourself." "Genesis 42 (King James Version)." Blue Letter Bible. Sowing Circle. Web. 25 Apr, 2015.

but Jacob said, "Go! Go; buy food. Then we will survive. Don't just stand there staring, starving. Take action."

When fears immobilize us, we would do well to heed Jacob's advice. Move. Do. Go. It is hard—just ask Joseph's brothers. But for them, doing nothing was akin to murder. The lives of their own children and grandchildren were at stake.

Jacob knew that his God is the God of life. Jacob knew God's promise to give Abraham as many descendants as the sand grains on the seashore. Sixty-six was just a beginning—there had to be more for them. Joseph was alive, and God was about to bring father and son together, although Jacob had no inkling of that. All Jacob knew was that he couldn't lose anyone to this famine. If it means going to Egypt, then go! Get moving. Now.

Although fear paralyzes, there are things we can do to overcome fear and live. There are actions we can take now. Gather to pray, to seek wise counsel, and then move! Act on the known information. Jacob reminds us that God will make a way. He may even have some surprises in store!

Honestly! Genesis 42:6–26

"We are honest men! We are brothers. We just want grain for our families. We are not spies. Honestly!"

The grain-master was insistent. He was gruff. What would it take to make him believe them? Little did the sons of Jacob know that the hard Egyptian governor before them was Joseph, the dreamer. "Sir," they begged, "we need grain for our families; that is the only reason we came."[17]

Joseph recognized his brothers instantly (Genesis 42:7). His gruff exterior and spy charge came as tests. Had they changed over the years, or were these the same ten who threw him into a pit? If given the chance, they might double-cross him and all of Egypt. How could Joseph know for sure that they were honest men? Would you trust them?

Talk is cheap, but Joseph was a quick thinker; a plan took shape. He put their claims to the test. First, he put his brothers in prison. The test was three days in prison. Three days to test their character, to observe their reactions, to see how honest they may or may not be. The second part of the test would be to send one brother home for Benjamin and continue to keep the rest in prison.

Joseph spent his three days with God. He listened to God. He modified the test. Joseph spoke to the ten on the third day. Crediting God[18] with the change of plans, Joseph's honesty test would allow

---

[17] Paraphrase of Genesis 42:10.
[18] See Genesis 42:17–20 and 50:20.

nine to go home with grain for their families. One man would remain behind in prison until the youngest brother arrived in Egypt.

Jacob's sons talked among themselves and agreed to this revision. They did not know Joseph understood their conversation; he used an interpreter to communicate with them at all times. The test worked. Joseph heard his brothers clearly. They told the truth. Let's listen in, too.

"This has all happened because of what we did to Joseph long ago. We saw his terror and anguish and heard his pleadings, but we wouldn't listen. That's why this trouble has come upon us" (Genesis 42:21).

Joseph's brothers thought they would die in Egypt because they had murdered Joseph. Nothing could be further from the truth—honestly! Joseph was overcome with emotion as his brothers passed this part of the test. Read his reaction in Genesis 42:23–24.

With Simeon secured as the guarantee of reunion with Benjamin, Joseph sent his brothers home with grain and other provisions. Maybe they were honest men, after all. Tune in next time for "So you paid for your grain, did you? The testing ain't over."

Oh No! Genesis 42

Oh no! You know the feeling. The hands-to-the-face moment you realize something has gone wrong, horribly wrong. Too often, you know your own choices and actions brought this on. Oh no. This heaviness of spirit belongs to every generation of human beings. It is without class, race, or any other barrier. Nearly two thousand years before Jesus was born, certain weary men felt the "oh no."[19]

They had had a rough go of it. They had encountered a particularly difficult Egyptian ruler. They spent three days in prison—one of them was still there. Now, though, the brothers stopped for a night's rest before resuming the journey home. The success of finally getting grain for their family was little consolation for all they had been through. What was it with that governor? His accusations—"You are spies!"—and endless questions about their father and younger brother wore the men out. Was this trip for food really worth all this trouble?

One brother opened a grain sack to feed the donkeys carrying the provisions. To his horror, he discovered his money pouch at the top of the sack. *Oh no!* His first question? "What has God done to us?" (Genesis 42:28)

These brothers, you see, were the very same men who had plotted to kill Joseph—one of their own flesh and blood. Despite modifying the plan when slave-traders happened by, Joseph's ten older brothers despised him; they thought of him as a nuisance, a brat. Funny, isn't

---

[19] Joseph's birth is listed as 1915 BC (not long after Stonehenge appeared in England) on the Complete Biblical Timeline PDF chart as found here: http://webminis.tyndale.com/chronologicallifeapplication/wp-content/themes/chronologicallifeapplication/clasb.pdf by Tyndale House Publishers, accessed 2/21/14

it, how the weight of unconfessed sin catches up to us. "Be sure your sin will find you out," Moses told the Israelites four hundred years later (Numbers 32:23 KJV).

Jacob's sons knew their sin; it found them out. "Terror gripped them" and Jacob as each son found his money in the grain sacks (Genesis 42:35). Simeon was in an Egyptian prison, Joseph was gone, and they could not return to Egypt for more grain without Benjamin. Sin has a way of growing, of destroying everything and everyone in its path. Oh no. Oh no. Oh no.

Jacob's sons had no way of knowing what the future held for them. They knew God was punishing them. They knew the heartache of dealing with the mess sin causes. The wages of sin is death (Romans 6:23). Death is painful. If you feel like Jacob, if the consequences of your actions and attitudes find you with your head in your hands, feeling dead, there is hope.

"If we confess our sins, he is faithful and just and will forgive us our sins and purify us from all unrighteousness" (1 John 1:9 NIV). Come clean, agree with God that we sin, and trust God to forgive and purify you. The *oh no* of Joseph's brothers was the first step in their confession and forgiveness. (We will see Joseph's forgiveness soon.) Awareness of sin comes before confession. Confession is essential to forgiveness. Cleansing follows forgiveness. And God is near to those who know they have sinned, to those whose hearts are broken by sin (Psalm 34:18).

Oh no gives way to the divine yes! Yes, it was good to go to Egypt for grain. Yes, it was good to encounter the rough ruler (better than the brothers could imagine). This famine brought Joseph's brothers down—oh no!—so God could lift them up—yes!

May the *oh no* moments of our lives cause us to face our sin, confess our sin, and be blessed with the divine yes!

It's Not about the Money

It's because of the money, thought Joseph's brothers. They came again to Joseph for grain, this time with Benjamin, as ordered. And again, things went far differently than they anticipated.

The man (Joseph) directed his household manager (do you suppose that man was as good at his job as Joseph had been in Potiphar's household?) to have the brothers eat the noon meal at his palace. Terror gripped the brothers. It must be about the money in their grain sacks from their last shopping trip. They didn't want to remember that awful experience!

Jacob had reluctantly permitted Benjamin to travel to Egypt. Benjamin was the treasure of his aged father's life. Releasing Benjamin, a father of ten sons of his own, broke the old man's heart.

Jacob sent gifts—the best of the land, including honey, spices, and nuts. Drought or not, Jacob was a wealthy man, and a generous one. Joseph's father sent money with his sons. Along with the payment for more grain, Jacob sent the price for the grain from the first trip—the cash they found in the top of their sacks. From his home and perspective, Jacob had no idea that it was not about the money.

The saga takes us directly to Egypt. The sons of Jacob found themselves at Joseph's home, afraid. The money in their sacks? Is that why they were there? Joseph's palace was a place of fear, the fear of slavery. Ironic, isn't it, that Joseph's brothers feared what they themselves had caused. All too often, what we fear or dislike in others is our own sin. Jesus calls this hypocrisy and warns us to get the logs out of our own eyes before worrying about specks in the eyes of others (Matthew 7:3–5). If the brothers only knew what Joseph was thinking.

This meal was about reunion—reunion and reconciliation. It wasn't about the money, guys! Our sin, whether against God or others, has the effect of keeping the focus on ourselves. Often, as with Joseph's brothers, the focus is fear—fear of what will happen to us. Sin causes my-opia. We cannot see beyond. We have no hope. We have dread—while Joseph had a party in mind. This is a "kill the fatted calf" moment! (Jesus' parables about being lost include the story of the son who squandered his inheritance. Hunger and fear forced him into a reunion, like Joseph's brothers. He, too, was greeted with a reunion meal. Read about it in Luke 15.)

"Relax." The household manager's response to the brothers' fear pointed them in the right direction (Genesis 43:23). Look to God, focus on the One who alone feeds and forgives. It's not about the money. It is about reunion and reconciliation with God! Look up, and let the party begin.

Relax!

Joseph's brothers were terrified at the prospect of going to Joseph's palace for lunch. Only reluctantly had Jacob agreed to send Benjamin along with them, and the weight of Benjamin's safe return rested on them. It would break their father's spirit if anything happened to him. And heading to the home of the hard man who insisted on their youngest brother's place with them scared them for another reason. Remember that money they found in their sacks on the way home the last time? They were sure they would be accused of stealing on top of everything.

The job of a household manager is to make things go smoothly and put guests at ease. Joseph knew the importance of a competent manager in an Egyptian household. He had done the job himself for Potiphar. He was good at his job—very good. Joseph expected the same loyalty and competence from his own manager.

A National Geographic video[20] of the inner workings of the White House during the presidency of Bill Clinton shows such a manager. One man was over all the many servants and assistants to President Clinton. That one man knew who, what, where, and when and made sure things ran perfectly—for every occasion.

So it was for Joseph's household manager. Joseph gave secret instructions to return the brother's grain price (Genesis 42:25). The manager may not have understood the reason for the refund, but he obediently saw to it that Joseph's order was enacted. On this day, when the brothers returned with Benjamin, he set in motion a

---

[20] (Geographic, 1998)

feast per Joseph's command. This efficient manager made sure that whatever Joseph wanted happened.

I can't help but wonder how this manager felt about Joseph's brothers. Did he look down on them because they were Hebrews? Though they brought gifts that indicated their own wealth on this second trip to Egypt, their travel weariness was evident. Did he feel somehow superior to them in his position? His master, after all, was the one whose planning and preparation rescued Egypt—and regions beyond—from the deadly famine. In a sense, Joseph died so his brothers could live. But a good household manager keeps his own feelings to himself and obeys orders. Joseph's brothers were afraid they would be accused of stealing. They told the manager so. He put them at ease. "Relax. Don't worry about it. Your God, the God of your ancestors, must have put it there. We collected your money all right," he told them (Genesis 43:23). He then offered customary hospitality to them and their donkeys.

Did you ever think about your position as a household manager? Those who believe in Jesus Christ are managers of the household of God. The Spirit of God dwells in you. Know you not you are the temple of the living God? (1 Corinthians 3:16) With God in us, we manage this household of faith—our own lives. How do we compare to Joseph, or his servant? We are to serve God obediently and faithfully. What matters is our attention to God's orders and wishes, whether we understand them or not.

Is someone you know terrified to come to God (like Joseph's brothers)? You are to put them at ease. Welcome them to the family of God. Make it as comfortable as possible for them to feast at the table with Jesus. Serve others with kindness and hospitality. Follow the instructions God gives you—whether they make sense to you or not. There are a host of hungry, weary people in need of reunion, forgiveness, and hope. Joseph's household manager followed orders and was instrumental in a family reunion with eternal results.

There is a great spiritual famine in our day. People will spend eternity separated from Jesus if you and I fail to be good stewards of the household of faith. Christ died that they might have life! God wants all people to be with him, to live with him for eternity. As servants of our Master, Jesus, we have much to offer! Today is the day to invite others in, to share God's hospitality. Our calling is to help others relax in the presence of Jesus.

Hospitality, Egyptian Style

We left Joseph's brothers in the care of the Egyptian. With refreshed feet and fed donkeys (Genesis 43:24), the men munched on fine fare in the palace dining room.

Although Egyptians and Hebrews did not eat together, this man seated the family as if he were one of them. He shared food from his own table, food in abundance—and you should have seen how much he gave Benjamin! If you left that table hungry or thirsty, it was your own fault. This was no peanut butter and jelly lunch for the sons of Israel (Jacob). It even beat macaroni and cheese!

Why the show of over-the-top hospitality? I wonder, so it seems likely that the brothers did as well. Water for feet and oil for the head were hospitality norms in Jesus's day. Imagine the refreshing feeling of cool water for hot, dusty feet. And though Joseph's brothers fell short on the care-for-the-kid-brother mark, they were able and attentive men who cared for their beasts of burden.

Reuben and the rest, descendants of Abraham, were on the cusp of fulfilling prophecy. God, when he passed between the cut halves of animals to covenant with Jacob's grandfather, told Abram (before his name change) that his seed would spend four hundred years as strangers in another nation, years of slavery (Genesis 15:13–14).

Strangers, or sojourners, are temporary inhabitants—just passing through. As such, strangers depend upon the kindness of others. Say you are suddenly on your own in a foreign country. You do not speak the language, nor do you know your way around the area or the customs. You are a stranger in need of hospitality! Now you know a tiny bit of how Joseph's brothers felt in Egypt, never mind the drama of the money returned in their sacks and this governor's rough treatment.

The New Testament calls believers in Jesus Christ to display hospitality. The Greek word hospitality is *philoxenia,* which means love of *(philo)* strangers *(xenia).* Believers are to entertain strangers (Hebrews 13:2), show hospitality without grudging (1 Peter 4:9), and in general, be given to hospitality (Romans 12:13). Jesus used himself as an example in Matthew 25. In the final judgment, God will collect those believers who cared for Jesus: "I was a stranger, and you took me in" (Matthew 25:35).

Joseph's Egyptian hospitality welcomed his brothers, fed them, and ministered to them as strangers. More than four hundred years later, another descendant of Abraham would issue instructions to be hospitable people. Moses passed on God's command to love strangers because "And now, Israel, what doth the LORD thy God require of thee, but to fear the LORD thy God, to walk in all his ways, and to love him, and to serve the LORD thy God with all thy heart and with all thy soul, to keep the commandments of the LORD, and his statutes, which I command thee this day for thy good?" (Deuteronomy 10:12–13 KJV) We love strangers because God loves us! Moses also reminded the Israelites to be hospitable because "you were strangers in Egypt" (Deuteronomy 10:19).

Hospitality is still the rule, even in other religions, although certainly lifestyles have changed from Joseph's day. An article in *Hiba Magazine* from November 12, 2012 entitled "Hospitality in Islam"[21] encourages hospitality even in today's society. Muslims believe that hospitality involves the host, the guest, and God. Believers in Jesus Christ have the same call to love the strangers (anyone who is passing through, anyone who is different, and anyone who needs a hand) in our midst.

---

[21] (Khan, 2012)

"Part of the goodness in hospitality is in receiving a person outside the community from whom one has no immediate expectation of reciprocity. The person you help may never be in a position to help you—he or she may even bring you harm. Still, hosts are obliged to extend themselves." [22] This quote from *The Extra Mile* by Miriam Schulman and Amal Barkouki-Winter in the Santa Clara University's Markkula Center for Applied Ethics reminds us who strangers are—those outside our normal circle of contacts.

How do we show love? During World War II, the Corrie ten Booms and Miep Gieses hid Jews (like Anne Franks). Not all of us have opportunities for such risky hospitality, though we do all have opportunities to care for others, and it might well pull us beyond our comfort zones. Hospitality may call us to share our lives with one whose political beliefs oppose our own. We may be called on to love the stranger whose lifestyle contradicts our senses. Perhaps the stranger demands more time than we want to give, or talks nonstop, or sulks no matter what we offer. Nevertheless, commanded to love we are—love as Jesus loves. Care as Jesus cares.

Joseph showed hospitality to his brothers, the very ones who wanted him dead. Can we do less?

---

[22] (Miriam Schulman and Amal Barkouki-Winter, 2000)

Family Order

Ruth, Lois, Keith, Ron, Karen.[23] Keeping five siblings in order may not be a great challenge, but try keeping a dozen boys in birth order! It's hard enough when all twelve have the same parents. I think of Frank and Lillian Gilbreth and their brood (efficiency expert Frank is a coauthor of *Cheaper by the Dozen*) or of the ten children of the von Trapp family. We have been following a family of twelve sons. The boys share the same father, but imagine trying to keep the birth order correct when four separate mothers are involved. Let's see if we can do it.

Reuben was the oldest of Jacob's boys. His mom was Leah. (She's the one whose dad tricked Jacob into marrying her.) Leah gave birth to more sons: Simeon, Levi, and Judah. Leah's sister Rachel was Jacob's choice bride. She wanted children badly but did not get pregnant, so she gave Jacob her maid, Bilhah, to bear the next children: Dan and Naphtali. The competition for children between the sisters heated up. Leah gave Jacob her maid, Zilpah, and Jacob fathered Gad and Asher. Rachel finally bore Jacob a son: Joseph. (You remember him!) Leah got pregnant two more times; Issachar and Zebulun came along. Leah also gave Jacob a daughter, Dinah, the only girl among twelve brothers! Lastly, Rachel was able to bear another son, Benjamin, but sadly, she died right after his birth. Okay, so did you follow that? Quick, put the boys in birth order at the dinner table.

Joseph did just that. He lined up his brothers from oldest to youngest at his Egyptian palace luncheon. Now remember, the brothers still thought Joseph was a hard man. They were terrified that this Egyptian invited them to lunch and more than a little spooked that

---
[23] My siblings graciously gave me permission to use their first names.

he lined them up this way. They were dumbfounded (Genesis 43:33). Even after seventeen years of separation from his family, Joseph remembered. Those who are from a large family always seem to know the order of their siblings, even if they are in early stages of dementia. I've heard the aged name off sisters or brothers with skill, even when most of the memory is gone. Like them, Joseph knew.

There is a basic need within us to be known. Though amazed at the place setting for this dinner from Reuben to Benjamin, Joseph's brothers must have been comforted to know that someone knew them. Before the days of text messages and internet searches, these guys were important. They were worthwhile. They were loved.

The same someone who knew and loved Jacob's sons—all twelve of them—knows and loves you. God was the someone behind the dinner in the Egyptian palace. He is also the One who went to great lengths to invite you to dinner, a feast prepared just for you! God knows all about you. He knows where you fit.

Joseph knew his brothers and what they had done wrong: yet he longed to eat with them. God knows our sin. And God longs for us to join him. He sets the table for our redemption through the death and resurrection of his only Son, Jesus. We are invited to feast with him if we are willing to believe Jesus is God and follow him. Twelve men ate with Jesus. Twelve turned away during Jesus's arrest and crucifixion, but eleven came back. The eleven chose to follow him, to live and die for him.

Joseph's brothers had more surprises waiting. God was preparing them for redemption and new life. The God of Jacob and his sons—and he knows them all by name—is the same God of Peter and Andrew, James and John, Philip, Bartholomew, Matthew, Thomas, James (son of Alphaeus), Simon the Zealot, Judas (son of James), and Judas Iscariot. God calls you to dinner, too. He loves for his family to surround him.

Joseph Shows Up

Joseph appears where and when you least expect him. I read a psalm a day. One day, I read Psalm 77, a psalm of Asaph, "for Jeduthun, the choir director." Lamenting the silence of God, the psalmist was overwhelmed, thinking God had forgotten him.

Have you ever felt forgotten by God? You are a believer. You live for Jesus. Your communion with God has been sweet up to a point—then you feel like your prayers suddenly hit a brick wall. It is almost as if God unexpectedly turned his back on you. What is going on? This was the psalmist's agony of heart. "I think of God, and I moan, overwhelmed with longing for his help" (Psalm 77:3). No sleep, too distressed to pray, memories of the good old days with God—these words of verses 4–5 are thoughts many believers know from personal experience.

A memory, fuzzy around the details, comes back. I went for a walk at dusk during an Asaph-like funk. My prayers were going nowhere. My heart was in agony. I couldn't understand why God was silent. Questions remained answerless. Did I offend God? I was unaware of anything specific. Was there hidden sin in my life? Perhaps, so I confessed both known and unknown, just in case. I literally wandered, wondering, headed nowhere specific. Beneath a streetlight that didn't yet yield much light, God let his light shine in my life once again. He hadn't left me after all. God was with me in my darkness. For me, it was a question of trust. Would I trust God no matter what I felt about his nearness? Yes, God, I will trust you, no matter what. You alone are trustworthy.

Joseph's release from the dungeon, his shower and shave moment, was no more dramatic than my streetlight moment. And Asaph? Asaph spent time thinking about all that God did in the past. He feared that God hated him; yet he could not stop thinking about the wonderful deeds God did in the past. Guess who showed up? Joseph. He was there for the psalmist in his dark spot, too! Well, actually, it was the God of Joseph who came through. You see, Asaph remembered the Red Sea miracle that redeemed the descendants of Jacob and Joseph. I think the question for the psalmist was a question of God's ability. Is God still able to deliver, to redeem?

Asaph pictured the waters when the Red Sea saw God (Psalm 77:16–18). God was so awe-filled (awful?) then, his presence so filled with thunder, lightning, and wind, that the sea had to run away. The sea fled, leaving a road, God's "pathway through the mighty waters" (Psalm 77:19). Joseph led the psalmist to the God whose power never fails, to the God who is still able to redeem.

Joseph's God is the psalmist's God and my God, too. Your need is unique and will determine your own question in your dark night of the soul (as some have described it).[24] Faithfulness for Joseph, God's ability for Asaph, and trust for me—yet the real question is always: will you cling to the I AM no matter what? Don't be surprised if Joseph shows up!

---

[24] (Cross, 1994)

Rejected!

Rejection. This bitter pill was the very one Jesus swallowed. Rejected by those he came to love, teach, and guide into new life, Jesus endured rejection over and over until it finally killed him. Though there is more to that story, we focus on his rejection as we look back in time.

I weep for Joseph's descendants. I weep for Joseph. Jacob and Joseph embraced when the old man finally arrived in Egypt. The reunion was all the sweeter because they had thought they would never get this chance again. Jacob met his Egyptian grandsons. Their haircuts and clothes were so different, yet even having never seen them before, Jacob loved Manasseh and Ephraim.

Jacob loved to bless those he loved. Barely out of the embrace with his Joseph, he blessed his son. Jacob blessed Joseph's boys, too. Joseph thought Jacob's poor eyesight mixed up his positioning of the lads. Older sons got the first blessing according to custom (unless you are Jacob and you steal the blessing from Esau—but that's another story). So why did Jacob bless Ephraim over Manasseh? Jacob himself answered our question. It was intentional, for "Manasseh, too, will become a great people, but his younger brother will become even greater. His (Ephraim's) descendants will become a multitude of nations!" (Genesis 48:19)

So why do I weep when I should be cheering? Time passed. God blew back the sea, and the roadway under the waters opened for the Israelites (remember, Jacob's new name was Israel, so his descendants got this name) to leave Egypt and move back home to the Promised Land. Jacob's blessing prediction had come true. Ephraim was great, and his descendants were many; they became warriors. The sad thing is that "they did not keep God's covenant, and they refused to live by his law" (Psalm 78:10). I weep for the broken faith, for the rebellion in Joseph's descendants.

Once in a while, a question comes to my mind, especially as I study Joseph and his integrity of spirit and faithfulness. Why did God choose Judah, and therefore David, for the lineage of Jesus? Why not Joseph? Psalm 78:9–12 reveals a character flaw in Joseph's younger son's family: they did not go to battle, even though they were warriors. They turned their backs on God. They forgot God's miracles. And they did not believe God (Psalm 78:22). So "God rejected Joseph's descendants; he did not choose the tribe of Ephraim" (Psalm 78:67). Just typing the word *rejected* is painful. If Ephraim's descendants had stayed close to Joseph's God, rejection would have cut them deeply. As it was, they didn't care. How sad. How very sad.

And I weep over them, broken for my hero and the sadness of his children walking away from the God he served and loved. I sob because I want faithfulness for the generations of my family. I cry for the lost potential, the futility of faithlessness.

Rejection from humans is hard to take. We know its sting, its devastation. Just imagine—is it even possible?—God's rejection. Oh, may it never be!

Hear our prayer, O Lord. Listen to our plea for our children, grandchildren, and to the thousandth generation. May they believe God, trust in Jesus, and stay loyal to you. May Jesus's rejection on the cross not be in vain. Oh, that our descendants might live in you and continue to remember all the miracles you have done, even back to Joseph and his family. Empower our children to live by your laws. Grant that the generations that follow us will stay faithful and obey you in everything. Help our descendants to teach their children of you so each new generation can set its hope on you once more. Oh, that our children will never experience your rejection, O God. Amen and amen.

Psalm 95 Prayer

Psalm 95 is about consequences, at least from the second half of verse 7 through the conclusion.

The Israelites made God angry through disobedience and hard hearts. Therefore, God did not let them enter the Promised Land, his place of rest.

That makes me wonder how many, if any, of Joseph and Jacob's descendants reached heaven. How many were eternally lost in forty years of wandering—how many actually kept on believing?

Yes, four hundred years of living in Egypt separated the Israelites from Joseph and Jacob. And yes, those who left Egypt had never known anything but Egypt, so the unknown Promised Land was scary and uncertain in their minds. The Egypt years exposed God's people to other gods, too. Even though they were slaves and life was hard—perhaps even impossible—they chose suffering in familiar settings over the unknown. Change is hard. "We never did it that way before."

I think of Joseph. He would have wanted his family to stay faithful. He would have wanted them to inherit the land of Canaan—the land of his father and grandfather, and the eternal Promised Land with God. I can almost feel Joseph's heartbreak when God said (about the Israelites), "They will never enter my place of rest" (Psalm 95:11).

I can't bear that any of my children and descendants would hear God say that to them, either. So, I pray.

Lord, for the generations that follow me, I ask you to help them stay faithful and obedient, whatever their circumstances may be. I pray for your power to keep them following Jesus even though the world around them goes other ways. I pray for Josephs, Davids, Deborahs, Ruths, and Pauls among them to win battles, to have integrity, to rise to the occasion, to go where you go, and to share the truth of Jesus Christ with others at all costs.

I pray that those who come after me will not make you so angry that you deny them rest (Psalm 95:10–11). I pray for forgiveness for my children and grandchildren and for a renewed commitment for them to know, love, and serve you. Provide Aarons and Hurs to lift their hands and heads in the hard places.[25] Provide eyes to see the host that is greater than the enemy when needed.[26]

Come to them when they are weary, and give them rest. Show them the right stones for their slingshots[27] when Goliath approaches. May their shots only come when they seek your honor and glory.

I plead for the blood of Jesus for the generations that follow me, Lord. May they hide themselves in you alone. Deliver them from evil. Help them choose wisely. Allow them enough struggles to become all they can be. Help them to stay faithful even in the wilderness experiences.

Your people in every generation have suffered, yet many become conquerors, victors through Jesus Christ. May it be so for those who follow me.

And Lord, Paul's prayer addresses his concern that he himself might fall away from you.[28] Keep me faithful and following Jesus, that my descendants will always know that you are Lord! You are I AM. Amen.

---

[25] Exodus 17:12
[26] 2 Kings 6:17
[27] 1 Samuel 17:40–50
[28] 1 Corinthians 9:27

Family Respect

"What kind of people do you think we are?" Joseph's brothers asked (Genesis 44:7). We react similarly when someone challenges us. Our reputation is at stake, the honor of our name. The family of Israel had God on their side. God's covenant with Abraham, the patriarch, made them special, unique. Did these Egyptians know with whom they were dealing?

Okay, so the sons of Jacob weren't perfect. They squabbled. They had killed men for the honor of their sister's name. (Dinah was raped, and they went ballistic [Genesis 34].) They were jealous, too. That's what got them all in the mess with these Egyptians. But they were Israelites, and that should mean something. They would not steal Joseph's silver cup. They even returned the money that had been in their sacks from the last grain-buying trip.

Back in the presence of Joseph, accused of another crime, Judah became the family spokesman. "Oh, my lord, what can we say to you? How can we plead? How can we prove our innocence?" Judah began his family defense humbly. "God must be punishing us," he said (Genesis 44:14–33). Family honor and the life of Jacob were on trial before Joseph. With fear, Judah explained the whole story to Joseph and begged for the freedom of Benjamin. Judah feared his father's death if Benjamin was held as a slave in Egypt. Judah had promised his father—his own word was at stake.

The honor of God's name, too, is at stake. Psalm 106 holds a litany of our failures to obey, to cling to Hashem (literally "the name," spoken by many Jews instead of "God") and to walk with God. We want respect; yet we fail to believe God. We desire the benefits of God's promises yet dig in our heels and refuse to go forward by faith.

Christians share the same heritage in Abraham as Jacob's family. God's covenant calls us to honor, obey, and live for the name; yet we are like Joseph's brothers. We do what we think is best instead of what God commands. We find ourselves in an Egypt-like slavery to our sins. We long for respect and honor while defaming God's holy name. As the apostle Paul said, we are most miserable apart from redemption.

We turn back to Judah. Responsibility coupled with realization brought Judah (and his brothers) to the point of humble confession. Here, finally, Jacob's family became respectable. At this point, Joseph broke down.

Do you suppose God breaks down when we finally come to our senses and humbly confess our sin before him? Hiding behind excuses and skirting responsibility do nothing for name or decency. It is at the point of repentance that we become respectable. God, being who God is, does not have an emotional collapse like Joseph when we repent. Yet there is great rejoicing when we—as individuals and as people—are honest before God. Our reputation and honor are at their best when they are hidden in God's reputation and honor. Now, that is family respect!

Together Again! Genesis 45:1-16

The world rejoices in happy reunions. An adopted child connects with a birth parent or siblings torn apart by war discover each other later in life. Joyful reunions bring a mixture of tears and joy. Coming together again after times of separation is the beginning of new life and new discoveries about loved ones.

Joseph's brothers, back before Joseph again because of a stolen silver cup, finally learned the truth about their brother. Once Joseph cleared the room of any Egyptian attendants, he sobbed, "I am Joseph."

The filming crew, had there been one that day, may have thought their sound equipment broke. The usually raucous brothers were too stunned to speak. Can you imagine the looks on their faces? Joseph's sobs grew louder—it seemed that all Egypt could hear him weep. "I am your brother, the one you sold. Come here."[29]

Joseph's joy infected his Egyptian family and friends. Pharaoh was happy for him. His brothers, on the other hand, were slow to warm up to this idea. Joseph's words, tears, and kisses helped to convince them, but there was an underlying fear in this reunion. Would there be some sort of revenge?

Joseph must have sensed their fear. He assured them that God led him to Egypt. God sent Joseph ahead of them so that their lives would be preserved. "Yes, it was God who sent me here, not you!" (Genesis 45:8)

---

[29] These are not direct quotes, but Joseph said these things to his brothers in his overall interaction with them in Genesis 45.

Joseph: Not Your Ordinary Joe

Joseph wanted his brothers to rejoice with him at this God-ordered reunion. And he wanted his father. This get-together, as climactic as it was, was incomplete. Jacob was not there yet. Joseph cared that his father and the family still back home would make it through the ongoing famine, but even more, he wanted to hug his dad. Twenty years is a long time to be separated.

"Dad will be surprised to see his son now," Joseph told his brothers. "Here I am, a ruler over all Egypt." We never know what God has in store for us. Our own life-paths may be convoluted and painful, but God has a purpose in it all. Rejoicing will come. One day, like Joseph, we will see how it all fits together for God's glory and our own good.

How many days and nights did Joseph anticipate this reunion day? How many prayers did he pray, and how many tears flowed in hopeful longing? God knows, and God made a way for our man of integrity and continued faithfulness—despite the pain and difficulty of his Egyptian circumstances.

There is a grand reunion in store for the family of God. One day, like Joseph's brothers, we will be face-to-face with Jesus—perhaps in stunned silence, or in exuberant weeping. God's joy will know no bounds. Heaven's rejoicing will know no end. Believers will be together again with the family of God forever. I'm so ready to be reunited with my Savior and my God. What about you?

If by the Spirit

"If, by the Spirit you put to death the deeds of the body, you will live" (Romans 8:13 NRSV). Joseph's brothers discovered this truth in Egypt. Joseph revealed himself to them. They wept together. Now, Pharaoh, the King of Egypt himself (can you imagine?), was ordering wagons, donkeys, and supplies for their journey back home to bring Jacob and all their wives and children down to live in Egypt for the duration of the famine. Pharaoh sent them off, saying, "Don't worry about your belongings, for the best of all the land of Egypt is yours" (Genesis 45:20).

One last trip lay ahead of them. One last reunion was to come. Eleven men set off, loaded down with new clothes (supplied by Pharaoh) and all they'd need for bringing their families—and especially their father—to live in Egypt. Joseph knew his brothers well, shouting his final, "Don't quarrel along the way!" as they rolled out of town (Genesis 45:24).

Starving, broken men had confessed their sin and found reunion. Now they were facing a king-sanctioned promising future—with Joseph! The sons of Israel literally went from death to life. Forgiven, fed, and clothed in righteousness, Joseph's brothers set out for a rescue mission—to bring Dad to Joseph, to bring him new life.

How awesome that our King—the ruler of the universe, Jesus Christ himself—provisions us! Wasting away in sin, desperate for hope, we are like Joseph's brothers. We show up bedraggled, hungry, and a mess. We confess our need first—because that is much easier than being honest about our sin. Not until the second trip (and even that took the arrest due to a silver cup in Benjamin's grain sack) did Judah finally confess the brothers' sins against Joseph. Coming clean—being honest about our own sins (and they are many)—is difficult. But we cannot move forward, we cannot truly live until we do. And "If we confess our sin, he is faithful and just to forgive us our sins, and to cleanse us from all unrighteousness" (1 John 1:9 KJV).

After we confess our sin to God we, too, need to put to death the deeds of the body. Putting quarreling to death was a need for the sons of Israel. What are some of the things you need to put to death? The promise is there that the Spirit will help us in that work, and that what follows is life. We, too, can be forgiven, fed, and clothed in robes of righteousness supplied by our King. That is truly something to celebrate!

I had never thought before about the Holy Spirit's role in Israel's new beginning, but the Spirit brought it to my attention as I read, and it was by the Spirit that Joseph's brothers put to death the deeds of the body, just as it is for us today. The promise of life for us post-New Testament believers was equally true for the Israel-sons, too. And I stand in awe of this awesome God of life. Holy, holy, holy LORD! Amen.

Standing Erect

So I'm studying Joseph, and his story gets interrupted by Genesis 38. What does his brother Judah's story have to do with Joseph—why the intrusion? Well ...

Judah picked out a bride for his son Er—a bad dude. Er died before the wedding. Law said Er's brother Onan must marry the girl—Tamar. The first boy would be in Er's name, right? Wrong. Onan spilled his seed on the ground to avoid any kids. Nice guy. Onan died childless, too. The third son, Shelah, was just a kid. Tamar had to wait until he grew up to get her baby. Wrong, again. Judah feared Shelah's death and conveniently forgot to call Tamar when he grew up.

It gets stranger. Time passed. Judah's wife died. He slept with who he thought was a prostitute but was actually Tamar. (Tamar took off her widow clothes when she knew he was in her area. He thought she was a prostitute, propositioned her for sex, and she agreed, with some strings attached). Zoom ahead three months. You guessed it; Tamar was finally pregnant with her father-in-law's child—but he didn't know that yet. Judah was outraged and called for her death (it was the law to stone prostitutes) until she revealed her secret.

So what does Tamar mean? To be erect, like a palm tree. And what did I learn? Tamar stood erect in the face of

- a wicked husband—snatched from her prematurely
- a conniving husband who cheated her from bearing a child
- a fearful father-in-law who denied her her last hope of marriage and children
- a two-faced father-in-law who had a double standard about sex

Joseph: Not Your Ordinary Joe

In the end, Tamar was the hero, bearing two sons (twins) who went on to be important in the lineage of Jesus.

Where does this leave us in the Joseph narrative? I see Tamar's likeness in Joseph, who stood erect in the face of his brothers' hatred, in the face of becoming a slave in Egypt, in the face of the lying wife of Potiphar, in the forgetfulness of jail mates whose dreams he interpreted. Joseph stood erect in his faith in God!

And us? We might get the short end of the deal, be cheated, lied about, forgotten, and raged against. But through faith in God we, too, can stand erect—and we have an advantage over Tamar and Joseph because we know that Jesus died in the same situation but rose to conquer sin and death. Thank you, Tamar. Thank you, Joseph. Thank you, Lord!

The Laughter Link

"They called him Laughter; for he came after the Father had made an impossible promise come true."[30] These words describe Isaac, Joseph's grandfather, whose name means laughter. Sarah's laughter was that of disbelief when his birth was promised and she was already eighty-nine years old. Her laughter turned to that of great joy when she held the son of promise in her arms.

Fast forward to the laughter of the Israelites (the descendants of Jacob). Although recently captives in Babylon, exiled far from home, they were back and able to worship in Jerusalem again! Psalm 126:1–3 describes their joy. "We were filled with laughter," says verse 2.

Between these outbursts of laughter were Jacob's life and Joseph's "death." We intersect Jacob as his sons returned from their second trip to Egypt. He heard their first words. "Joseph is still alive!" He was stunned, unable to laugh or cry at the news. Evidence, in the form of wagons loaded with supplies, convinced Jacob. "My son Joseph is alive!" (Genesis 45:26–28) "A merry heart doeth good like a medicine" (Proverbs 17:22 KJV). Jacob's spirits lifted with hope. Imagine his joy.

Interesting thing, this joy that links the patriarchs. Nearly always born in adversity and dark days, joy comes in the morning and surprises us. Sarah did become pregnant and give birth—at ninety! Joy! Jacob did see Joseph again—we'll soon see the reunion. The Israelites did come back to Jerusalem. Joy, joy, joy!

---

[30] (Card, 1989)

Hold on when your laughter is filled with bitterness and disbelief—like Sarah's. Hold on when tears and agony of spirit mark your Jacob-like days. Keep on keeping on when you feel isolated and forgotten like the Israelites in Babylon. Joy is just around the corner, and you will laugh again. The same God who made impossible promises come true in the past is God today. He is still the joy-bringer. Prepare for the journey of a lifetime with Jacob. We'll soon meet him in Egypt. A merry heart is good medicine.

Jacob and His God

He was about to set out on a journey to Egypt. In all his travels, Jacob had never been to that country. He was an old man, and travel was more challenging. Still, Jacob was set on this journey. He wanted with everything in him to see his eleventh son. How long had it been since he hugged Joseph? Too long! But the trip ahead ...

One thing Israel (as he is now known) knew was that God was with him. He remembered other journeys. Once, he fled his home, fearful when his brother Esau was so angry. Sure, he was on the way to his uncle's—but they didn't know each other. With a stone for a pillow, Jacob settled one night. The God of his grandfather and father came to him in a dream with angels going up and down stairs between earth and heaven. That's pretty neat!

At the top of the stairway stood the LORD, and he said, "I am the LORD, the God of your grandfather Abraham, and the God of your father, Isaac. The ground you are lying on belongs to you. I am giving it to you and your descendants" (Genesis 28:13).

I am the LORD. I am Jehovah. I am Yahweh. I AM that I AM. Jacob's encounter with God was amazing. Are you overcome with God's self-revelation to Jacob? Here's a deceitful man who stole his father's blessing, on the run to who knows where, and the I AM God stopped to introduce himself. Not only that, the LORD told Jacob, "I will be with you, and I will protect you wherever you go" (Genesis 28:15). Oh, and if that were not enough, God told Jacob he would finish "giving you everything I have promised." Jacob named that dream place Bethel, which means house of God. Did he shake his head in the morning? Did Jacob have to pinch himself? He just had an encounter with the covenant God of Abraham and Isaac.

Joseph: Not Your Ordinary Joe

His thoughts drifted again Jacob and his burgeoning family were leaving Laban. He told his wives, "God has been with me" (Genesis 31:5). Jacob knew God protected him from Laban's many deceits. Near the end of that journey, Jacob found himself in an overnight wrestling match. Holding on for a blessing, Jacob came away with both a blessing and a new name—Israel. In awe again, Israel declared, "I have seen God face to face" (Genesis 32:30).

Memories filled Joseph's father with confidence. No matter how long or difficult the trip to Egypt might be, Israel would once again hug his son, and his God would be with him!

God reveals himself to us, too. God will meet you in the journey of life, often when you feel least deserving. There was the time I knew the ugliness of my sin. How could anyone love me, least of all God? Yet it was then, at one of the darkest times of my life, that God led me to the Song of Solomon: "You are altogether beautiful, my darling; there is no flaw in you" (Song of Solomon 4:7 NIV). How could God say that to me, I wondered? Yet, the assurance came so sweetly, and it still brings tears to hear him tell me now.

My prayer for you—as you read this, and as you journey through life, whatever your paths may be—is that God will reveal himself to you in ways that keep you going, that lift your spirits or push you out of your ruts. May you move ahead with the confidence of Jacob, knowing that God is with you. May you know for certain that God will keep his promises in your life, even if you are setting out on yet another difficult expedition.

Grace at Work

Joseph's family increased while they lived in Egypt. They started small—it is so like God to begin with next to nothing. Things were great at first—well, except for five remaining years of famine, but they had food, and they were all together. Goshen was fertile, and so were the Israelites. The Pharaoh paid little heed to Joseph's kin. They were shepherds, after all.

The Israelites had each other. The isolation of Egypt kept them from marrying Canaanites and kept their bloodline pure. More importantly, the separation kept their faith pure, undiluted by the worship of the many Canaanite gods.

The trouble was that living in Egypt was not exactly paradise. And as the clan increased into the size of a nation, the Egyptian powers that be grew increasingly fearful of revolt from within. Freedom became slavery. Slavery led to earnest prayer. Prayer paved the way out. You remember, the sea blew back, and the slaves became free again. This, my friends, is grace in action! Grace is not limited by how things look or by powers that be.

Grace—God's unmerited favor—is marvelous, always at work behind the scenes. Just think: the same grace at work in Israel's four hundred years of Egyptian slavery is still at work today.

Are you enslaved in some way? Grace is at work. When the time is just right, you will be amazed. Keep your faith pure, undiluted, and uncompromised. Keep your eyes on Jesus.

Joseph's family grew from about seventy-five in number to a nation of over six hundred thousand during the Egypt years. They were ready to take possession of Canaan, the land of God's promise. Get ready for your own Promised Land! Grace will get you there.

The Embrace of a Lifetime Genesis 46:29

It was a miracle! After thinking Joseph was dead, Jacob finally held Joseph in his arms. They wept together "for a long time," Scripture records (Genesis 46:29). The embrace erased thirty years in a moment. Here they were, father and son, finally face to face again, and it seemed like it happened so fast.

Jacob, at age 130, felt a satisfaction like nothing he had felt before. The hug with Joseph finally convinced him that his son was alive. Jacob held on, not wanting the moment to pass.

A soldier returns from war. A daughter graduates from college. A husband dies. A son comes to his senses and comes home to his father's embrace—"But while he was still a long way off, his father saw him and was filled with compassion for him; he ran to his son, threw his arms around him and kissed him" (Luke 15:20 NIV). Embraces of relief, celebration, and comfort—they communicate more than words at special times.

This was an embrace of resurrection. "'For this son of mine was dead and is alive again; he was lost and is found.' So they began to celebrate." Though Jesus was talking about God's joy over the repentant sinner, he also perfectly described Jacob's joy in his parable of the Prodigal Son in Luke 15:24. (Aren't the ties between the Old and New Testament awesome?) Joy is like that!

Jacob's joy overflowed into blessings. He blessed Pharaoh twice when Joseph presented him to the Egyptian king. Jacob blessed his sons. He blessed Joseph's sons. Jacob was joyful in the blessing of the embrace of a lifetime. The psalmist said, "Weeping may endure for a night, but joy comes in the morning" (Psalm 30:5b NKJV). This joy remained with Jacob throughout his final seventeen years—with all his family together.

The God of Jacob and Joseph longs to embrace you and fill you with joy. Like Jacob, God wants all his children living with him, forever!

The Remnant of Joseph *Amos 5*

It's awfully hard to watch someone you love go through hard times. It's so hard to see loved ones choose unwisely or blindly and suffer as a result of those choices. Joseph's family multiplied in Egypt. They became a great nation, and he saw benefits and blessings in the remainder of his lifetime. But things had changed by the time of the prophet Amos. Would Joseph have agonized to see the remnant of his family in Amos's day? I think so.

The house of Joseph (I wonder why Amos focused on Joseph as he prophesied), also known as the family of Jacob, dwindled drastically from the Exodus-sized multitude. Amos called them a remnant. Think residue, remains, or leftovers. Can you imagine how Joseph might have felt had he seen the sorry shape of his family? That he did not see their sorry state was a gift of God's grace. Joseph rode the wave of faithfulness and obedience. God blessed Joseph beyond measure. The trouble was that his kin did their own thing instead of seeking Joseph's God. The house of Joseph forgot to listen, ignored what they did hear, and only acted on parts they liked. This sounds like some parts of the body of Christ today. We enjoy our "have it your way" culture even in worship. We forget the God of our salvation unless we are in over our heads.

Seek God, oh family of Joseph. Seek God and live (Amos 5:14–15). Nearly one thousand years after Joseph's death, Amos intended to shock Joseph's descendants with his lament over their wayward living. They were in over their heads and didn't even realize it.

A lament is an expression of grief: it is mourning. Amos predicted death for the remnant of Joseph. He sang over them as if they had already died. Maybe we need to sing over some churches, some branches of the body of Christ today.

You just never know where Joseph might show up. Maybe there is still time for the house of Joseph. Maybe a funeral dirge might be enough to change the course of our history. Do you lament the sin-sickness around you? Does injustice precipitate the song of Amos within you? Is your family in danger of disappearing—eternally—for ignoring the I AM God? Sing with Amos. The remnant of believers in our own day and age need to hear and heed the lament.

You see, God sees us, the remnant of Joseph. He sees our waywardness, our refusal to obey. God agonizes over the destruction we bring upon ourselves. Who will be our Amos? Who will sing death's song over us? Yet there is hope in the refrain: seek God and live. Those words of Amos are hope-filled words.

Oh, house of Joseph, seek God and live. Today, before it is too late, search for God. Oh, church of Jesus Christ, you who are descended from the family of Abraham, Isaac, Jacob, and Joseph, turn your hearts toward the One who can rescue you and your loved ones from extinction. Remnant of Joseph, seek God and live!

Meanwhile

My coworkers frequently hear me say, "Meanwhile, back at the ranch …" My grandfather loved westerns. My dad loved westerns. I usually repeat the dusty phrase after something has interrupted the flow of my work—you know, after the cows stampeded or after bandits robbed the stage.

Moses[31] wrote of Joseph, "Meanwhile, the famine became worse" (Genesis 47:13). You see, the arrival of Joseph's family, their meeting with Pharaoh, and their settling-in phase in Goshen broke up the narrative of Egypt's seven-year famine.

Now, back at the ranch—the worsening famine. Moses showed us Joseph and his God-given management abilities. Egyptians used cash for food until that ran out. Listen as they cried to Joseph in verse 15: "Our money is gone! Why should we die?"

Joseph suggested buying food with livestock. And so many Egyptians did that, Moses noted, that all of Egypt's horses, flocks, herds, and donkeys became Pharaoh's possession in that year of the famine.

People sold themselves and their land to Joseph the next year. "Just give us grain so that our lives may be saved" (verse 19). I have never been so desperate for food that I considered selling myself as a slave. What must it feel like to be that scared and hungry? Where is hope?

---

[31] Most scholars credit Moses with writing the first five books of the Bible. It is my conviction that God revealed the whole of the story to Moses during his forty days and nights on the mountain with God, although the Hebrew tradition of retelling the story gave Moses a relatively complete picture to begin with. I imagine Moses, after his recording session was complete, wondering about all God revealed. Was Joseph one of Moses's heroes? I will ask him when I get to heaven.

Joseph: Not Your Ordinary Joe

Meanwhile, back at the ranch, Joseph was cooking up deliverance for the Egyptians. He shared seed for the future, enough to plant when it rained and the famine ended. From that first planting, the Egyptians had enough to eat and enough to use for seed the following year. Finally!

While Joseph was busy saving the lives of the Egyptians, things were looking up for Jacob, too. "So the people of Israel settled in the land of Goshen in Egypt. And before long, they began to prosper there, and their population grew rapidly" (Genesis 47:27). Jacob lived out his remaining seventeen years in the relative comfort Goshen afforded.

God is in our meanwhile, too. While you are distracted with joys[32] or sorrows, with problems or unexpected solutions, God is at work—like Joseph—planning, making preparations, and saving lives. Thanks be to God!

---

[32] The birth of our newest grandson, Nathaniel, has been a joyous distraction in our lives, and this grandmother goes back to the ranch with pictures!

Joseph's Oath *Genesis 47:27-31*

"Promise me!" There was urgency in Jacob's voice. "Promise me, Joseph," he begged. Genesis 47 ends with Jacob's plea: "If you are pleased with me, swear most solemnly that you will honor ... my last request." He needed Joseph's oath.

What weighed so heavily on Jacob's mind? Why was it so important that Jacob insisted, "swear that you will do it" (Genesis 47:31)? And why did Jacob need Joseph to swear—to vow that he would keep his promise?

An oath is powerful. "Do you swear to tell the truth?" we ask a courtroom witness. We expect those taking the oath of office to fulfill their vow to uphold the laws of the land. Abraham's servant Eliezer vowed to bring home a wife for Isaac (Jacob's father) from among relatives, and he brought home Laban's sister, Rebecca.

So what demanded this oath? "Take me home." Jacob wanted his bones buried in the Cave of Machpelah, Abraham's cave—home. Abraham bought the piece of ground from Ephron and the Hittites when Sarah died. Though it was offered as a gift, Abraham purchased the property, paying top price for the field and trees that surrounded the cave near Mamre, even if it was not all that valuable.

> So Ephron's field in Machpelah near Mamre—both the field and the cave in it, and all the trees within the borders of the field—was deeded to Abraham as his property in the presence of all the Hittites who had come to the gate of the city. Afterward Abraham buried his wife Sarah in the cave in the field of Machpelah near Mamre (which is at Hebron) in the land of Canaan. So the field and the cave in

it were deeded to Abraham by the Hittites as a burial site. (Genesis 23:17–20 NIV)

Joseph listened to the passion in his father's voice and heard the cry of his heart. Jacob knew he would die soon, but Isaac and Abraham lay buried in the land of promise. There is something sacred to a grave, especially one back home. Like Abraham and Isaac, Jacob trusted God's promise. He believed with all his heart that one day, his sons and their families would possess Canaan and live there as the nation of Israel. "Please, Joseph, please."

Have you ever been where the remains of a beloved grandparent lay? Have you felt the special connection there? Brookhouser Hill is such a place. I feel close to my grandpa when I visit there. His stone says J. F. Morris, but he signed his name "Granddad." Jacob felt it stronger now—Machpelah called out to him. His time on earth was nearly over. He just had to lie with his father and grandfather in that cave, that cave back home.

It mattered to Jacob. It was so vital that he demanded his son's oath. So Joseph promised, and his oath set Jacob's mind at ease because they both trusted the God of promise and fulfillment. Joseph took his oath with every intention of keeping his vow. And when the time came, he did take Jacob's bones back home—home to the Cave of Machpelah, home to the land that the God of promise did, indeed, return to the Israelites—just as he had promised.

He Sat Up in Bed Genesis 48

It was Joseph's last visit with his father. Jacob was dying. Ephraim and Manasseh waited in the background.

During my years as a hospital chaplain, I saw many families surround a dying loved one. Teenagers rarely come for the vigil, but of those who do come, few stay close to the failing one. Even when a parent or grandparent is dying at home, teens hang back. Death is painful and difficult to watch. How surprising it would be to see that weakened one sit up!

Ephraim and Manasseh were never close to their grandpa. Born in Egypt and raised as Egyptians, Joseph's sons were different in every way—except that Joseph reared his sons in the faith of God as his father had raised him. It's no wonder they resisted coming close to the bed of Jacob as he neared his passing. I wonder what they were thinking. They had no Gameboy or iPad, and certainly no cell phone with them to distract them from death's shadow. Did they ask Joseph, "Dad, why do we have to go?" Maybe their whine "but we barely know him" was loud enough for Jacob to hear. On the other hand, maybe they did really want to be there but were totally uncomfortable once they arrived. We know they hung back because Jacob had to ask Joseph to bring them to him (Genesis 48:9).

Jacob was dying, but he wasn't dead yet! In fact, when Joseph and the boys arrived, he "gathered his strength and sat up in bed" according to Genesis 48:2. Jacob had important work ahead of him even then. He had to see Joseph and his grandsons one more time. His mission was to bless them with a blessing that would last for eternity. It is rare for a dying man to sit up in bed, although it happens. It's even rarer for that man to speak more than a few words. However, there is power in the spoken blessing—empowerment for speaker and receiver. (Try it! You surely don't have to wait for your deathbed!)

Jacob remembered his own blessing (Genesis 28:10–22). God's promise to be forever with Jacob sent him on his journey to find a wife. The sanction and power of God's presence was the blessing Jacob felt the undeniable urge to pass on. With strength not his own, Jacob raised himself up.

It was an awkward moment—the blessing. Manasseh and Ephraim were not babies. Jacob lived seventeen years in Egypt, so Joseph's sons were in their late teens or early twenties; yet Jacob treated them like youths. He blessed his kneeling grandsons as if they were his very own sons. You might expect them to be thrilled. You might think Joseph would be happy. And you might be wrong. The dying man on a mission is not out to please others. He does what he must no matter the reaction. Joseph's sons failed to react—at least, Scripture is silent. Joseph, however, was distressed. Jacob mixed the boys up. Ephraim got the blessing of the older son, but he was the younger (Genesis 48:13–14). But it was no mistake. Jacob knew what he was doing (Genesis 48:19–20).

Death hurts. We don't react well. The simple things can upset us—wrong wording in an obituary, Aunt Susie's salad isn't here for the dinner, that kind of thing. So it was for Jacob's blessing. But it is okay.

Jacob sat up. He blessed Joseph through his sons. The blessing remains. We will get through it, just as Joseph did, and life goes on. Think resurrection! Thanks be to God!

Appropriate Blessings Genesis 49

Jacob wasn't blind. Oh, his sight was nearly gone, but his powers of insight were sharp! Jacob knew his sons. He observed what kind of person each one was throughout his life. Fathers need to know their sons and daughters. Jacob did.

Each of Jacob's sons received a blessing on the day Jacob died. He spoke a blessing appropriate for each son (Genesis 49:28), a blessing that fit the man. Take time to read each one, listed chronologically in Genesis 49, and get a feel for who each was.

What blessing would be appropriate for a murderer? Read Jacob's blessing for Simeon and Levi in verses 5–7. Jacob knew the shenanigans of his boys. He remembered their excessive rage over their sister's rape, how they murdered a whole town of men for the deeds of one man. As I read, I wonder how Jacob's blessing would affect these sons in the future. Before my whole question tumbles out, the Holy Spirit answers. God chose Levi and his sons to be the priests. Remember Aaron?

At first reading, it doesn't sound much like a blessing: "Cursed be their anger, for it is fierce; cursed be their wrath, for it is cruel. Therefore, I will scatter their descendants throughout the nation of Israel" (verse 7). Yet Jacob's blessing set the stage for God to have passionate men everywhere. The men themselves were not cursed, only the dangerous emotions that plagued them and goaded them to sinful violence. And the consequence of their sin, the dispersion of their descendants throughout Israel, was God's plan to have the tribe of priests, men passionate about purity and God's way, intermingled throughout his people for their good. Jacob saw the good, even in these, his sons who were men of violence. So he blessed them.

Jacob teaches us how God sees his children. In a large family like Jacob's, there are a variety of personalities and characteristics—and every single one has worth. We may not be "a fruitful tree beside a fountain" like Joseph (verse 22), but we may be strong like Issachar or able to produce "magnificent fawns" like Naphtali. Perhaps there are governors among us like Dan—beware passers-by (verse 17). God even knows those of us who love the sea like Zebulun (verse 13).

We may think we pull the wool over the eyes of our parents. Or we may think they fail to notice our good deeds. Joseph's father, about to breathe his last, shows us our parents do know us—and even if they do not, God does. Each of us receives a blessing appropriate to who we are. And God uses those blessings for good, even if we are a Simeon or a Levi! Hallelujah!

Blessing is powerful. Jacob's blessing to his violent sons changed the course of their future and impacted all of the nation of Israel in the process. Don't neglect to speak words of blessing to those around you—even (perhaps especially!) to those who are a little rough around the edges. You never know what transformation God intends to accomplish through that blessing. Double hallelujah!

Blessing Primer

"Sticks and stones may break my bones, but words can never hurt me." So goes a saying from my childhood. It's a lie, of course! Words can hurt us deeply—but there is good news. Words can also be a blessing. Merriam Webster's online dictionary definition of blessing includes the line, "approval that allows or helps you to do something."[33] Blessing also indicates favor. Blessings are words that build people up rather than tear them down. Blessing words equip us to follow Jesus, to take up our crosses, to live more fully. We all need to hear words of encouragement and words that build us up.

Just how do you bless others? What do you say? How do the experts do it? Let's listen in on Jacob's blessings. He practiced the art frequently. Jacob stated truths, observed qualities, commended strengths, offered prayers for the future, and celebrated the God who blessed him as he blessed his sons and others.

Observant parents realize that each child is unique. There is no "one size fits all" blessing. If you and I are to bless our children and grandchildren—and we must, for everyone needs blessing—we must tailor the blessing. Fortunately, Jacob gave us a blessing primer! Genesis 49 records words of prophecy and promise that Jacob spoke over each of his sons. His twelve sons remind us of the twelve disciples of Jesus, so different from each other, each with his own strengths and weaknesses.

Jacob observed the qualities of each of his sons over the years. He stated truths about each one in his blessings over them. Jacob commended their strengths; he offered individual prayers for his

---

[33] (Merriam-Webster Online Dictionary, 2015)

boys. Jacob celebrated the God of promise and power he knew so well, desiring that all twelve of his sons would have an individual relationship with this same God. And Jacob was specific—what he asked of God was unique to the son for whom he prayed. Jacob gave each son a blessing that was appropriate.

Look around you for someone to bless today. What do you observe? In your words over them, state truth. Commend the strengths you see, and pray for help in overcoming weakness. Offer prayer for the future—what do you see them accomplishing? Celebrate God for who he is in and through the person you wish to bless. Finally, be specific. Remember that while a "God bless you" may be appropriate for someone who sneezed or may serve as words of thanks, the phrase is vague at best, one Jacob avoided.

Let's say you want to bless the bus driver. You sat behind her every day for six years of secondary education. You watched her shift gears smoothly and noticed how she used her feet effectively on the clutch and brake. You decide to write to her. You might first thank her for her many years of service and her patience in dealing with students—you tell her that you remember some of the shenanigans aboard the bus. You might then tell her what you noticed in her abilities and let her know that she taught you to drive because of what you observed. Finally, you bless her in her retirement that she may continue to be the deft person she has been. You tell her you are praying for God to help her keep her good coordination skills in the navigation of life, whatever obstacles and challenges she might face.

Be a blesser like Jacob. He's a good teacher. Follow his example—state truths, observe qualities, commend strengths, offer prayer, celebrate the Almighty, and be specific in your requests. Both you and your recipient will be glad you did!

Faith of Our Fathers

"Oh, my papa, to me he was so wonderful." The line wove its way through my head this morning. I wonder if Joseph might have sung it, too.

Joseph's unfinished story has worked its way through my thoughts and prayers. I wondered how to properly bring our time with Joseph to a close. My wonderful Papa (our Father) revealed the answer in Hebrews 11:22.

Hebrews 11, as you probably know, is all about faith and our fathers of faith. Abraham gets a lot of press. No wonder. His faith was amazing! God texted Abraham. "Meet me over there." Huh? Oh. Okay! Abraham set out with no GPS. He got there and found no inn, not even a stable, so he set up his tent.

Camping is fun for a while—unless it rains or there is strong wind or sandstorms (like there). Can you imagine tenting it for years—for generations? Not so fun. Yet Joseph's fathers Abraham, Isaac, and Jacob all lived in tents. They didn't even own the campground! Hebrews 11:16 explains, "They were looking for a better place." God promised Abraham a homeland, and Abraham believed God. Abraham and his descendants looked for more than a piece of ground to build a new house. They looked forward to a "city with eternal foundations, a city designed and built by God" (verse 10). Our fathers of faith were nomads on earth because this earth is not the Promised Land.

Joseph neared his death in Egypt, far from the land of Canaan— the land of his youth, the land we call the Promised Land. He was certain, beyond a shadow of doubt, that God would one day lead the

Israelites back there. He commanded that his bones be carried back there, but even the cave at Machpelah—the only ground Abraham ever owned, where his bones were buried—was not home. Joseph, too, was a nomad on this earth, although he lived much of his life in a palace instead of a tent.

Joseph's faith was strong, like Abraham's. His confidence was in what he did not see. Was it worth it? Hebrews 11:13 says, "All these faithful ones died without receiving what God had promised them." If it ended there, we might be tempted to give up on God, to quit believing. But there's more: "[T]hey saw it all from a distance and welcomed the promises of God." Nomads who look forward to more, verse 14 assures, are "looking forward to a country they can call their own"—a better place.

Rarely do we know what is going on behind the scenes. But when we trust the One who is working in the unseen, like Abraham and Joseph, we have confidence that it will all work out for our good, so we can run with the promises. The certainty in Joseph's "take my bones with you" directive was that God would indeed make a way. And he did (Joshua 24:32)!

Albert Brumley's 1937 song might have been Joseph's. The lyrics say,

> This world is not my home,
> I'm just a-passing through.
> My treasures are laid up
> Somewhere beyond the blue.
>
> The angels beckon me
> From heaven's open door,
> And I can't feel at home
> In this world anymore.

Ruth Ann Moore

>Oh Lord, you know
>I have no friend like you.
>If heaven's not my home,
>Then Lord, what will I do?
>
>The angels beckon me
>From heaven's open door,
>And I can't feel at home
>In this world anymore.
>
>Just over in Gloryland,
>We'll live eternally.
>The saints on every hand
>Are shouting victory.
>
>Their songs of sweetest praise
>Drift back from heaven's shore,
>And I can't feel at home
>In this world anymore.
>
>Oh Lord, you know
>I have no friend like you.
>If heaven's not my home,
>Then Lord, what will I do?
>
>The angels beckon me
>From heaven's open door,
>And I can't feel at home
>In this world anymore.

Joseph died in Egypt, but God beckoned him to live in that eternal city not built by human hands. I plan to look him up when I get there. I have so much to ask him, so much to catch up on.

Here's the question for us: if we have the faith of our fathers (and it is my prayer that we do), and if we believe that this world is not our home (and that's harder for some of us than others), then what are we doing now to prepare ourselves and future generations for the Promised Land? Winford Claiborne, a Bible study writer, asks, "Since this world is not our home, are you preparing for the home Jesus Christ has promised to the faithful?"[34]

Whether a vacation trip or a move to another home, earthly journeys involve packing. Our journey to heaven differs. We cannot take anything external with us. (And thankfully, there are no X-ray machines to endure.) But prepare we must. Check your relationship with God. Review the traveling orders (God's Word), and follow the instructions. Bring the one essential, the only thing you can bring along: your trust in Jesus. What are you doing to get ready to go home? Joseph, like Abraham, packed his faith, and that was enough!

---

[34] http://www.gospelhour.net/2288.html

Epilogue

My journey with Joseph brings us right back to where we started. A young man, forsaken by his brothers, learned a powerful lesson. Joseph thought he was alone. He was in the pit when he learned about the I AM presence of God. God's withness accompanied Joseph into Egyptian slavery and stayed with him in the darkest dungeon days of his life. God never left Joseph! Nor did Joseph leave God.

Joseph learned to trust God's presence, to live out of his confidence. His faith did not waver. Joseph died at age 110, fully trusting in the I AM God of Abraham, Isaac, and Jacob.

Joseph made the most of every experience—the positives and the negatives. He used his mind and heart in serving others. Joseph was a blessing, walking in the footsteps of Jacob and his ancestors.

I have learned from my study of my hero Joseph. I thought I would see a man of integrity. I did. I thought my study would remind me of Joseph's confidence that God uses all things for good—saving lives. It did. I was not aware of how amazing Joseph was. I felt like I was growing up with him. Maybe I did. I feel like I could start all over and gain a thousand new insights. Maybe I will. One thing is certain; Joseph is not your ordinary Joe. What I know is that Joseph and his awesome God mean more to me now than ever before.

It is my prayer that you will want to know this God—the promise keeping, constantly present God of Joseph—in greater detail. Keep digging!

Read the Word, learn the Word, live the Word.

Afterword: Resurrection, Joseph Style
Genesis 45:4-8

Sometimes it is hard to put words to God's revelations. This one blows me away. Before Jesus was born, before he died, we find glimpses of the resurrection in the Old Testament. In particular, we see one of those glimpses in my hero, Joseph. Let's peek in.

Joseph repeated himself three times in these short verses, saying to his brothers, "God sent me here ahead of you." "Here," of course, was Egypt. You know the story. Joseph dreamed. His brothers got jealous. They sold him. (At least they didn't kill him!) He worked as a slave for Potiphar. His work got him a promotion to household manager. Mrs. Potiphar lusted and then lied, and Joseph found himself in the dungeon. Three years and three dreams later, he got his rags to riches break. Then Joseph doled out grain. It was all part of the master plan. Two years into a seven-year famine, and who was in line for grain again? That's right, Joseph's brothers!

They had no idea who this harsh Egyptian official really was. Joseph knew them right away on their first trip. He roughed them up a bit, though not with fists: he accused them of spying. It was his way of testing them—and he really wanted to see Benjamin.

With Benjamin in tow, the brothers eleven stood before Joseph again. They still didn't recognize him. He walked like an Egyptian, erect, with little trace of his shepherding roots. Once again, Joseph was hard on the sons of Jacob until he could stand it no longer.

The whole palace of Pharaoh heard Joseph weeping during the big reveal. And suddenly, instead of joy, terror overtook the men. "Come near," Joseph urged. "I am your brother." Imagine the shock! To the eleven, Joseph did not look like a son of Jacob. Neither did he sound like one.

Think of this, though. Up until then, Joseph spoke through an interpreter to his brothers. They spoke Aramaic. He used the Egyptian tongue. I imagine this scene with Joseph speaking their language. "Come near. I speak your language because I am one of you. I have good news for you." This, my friends, is certainly resurrection. And (despite the brothers' fears), resurrection is good news!

Resurrection, Joseph style, is news that life will go on, that hope is not dead! "God sent me before you to preserve life." God sent Joseph. This is the exact message they needed to hear and hear again. Joseph's place and position in Egypt were God's plan for their salvation. This reveal was no less dramatic than Jesus's whispered "Mary"[35] outside the empty tomb. Joseph, at least in the eyes of his brothers, rose from the grave. He was alive!

The cross in all its horror and humiliation was God's plan! Had Jesus remained in the tomb, had there been no resurrection, there would be no hope. Mary, the Magdalene woman once set free from demons by grace and Jesus's power, came to the tomb in the dark that morning. The darkness outside matched her cold, dark soul. Jesus had rescued her, healed her. Now he was—wait, he was gone?! The tomb was empty. "Risen," the angels reported—but what is that?

That, my friends, is a twelfth brother who speaks Jacob's language but doesn't look like he used to. I imagine that Joseph's tongue was as tender with the name Benjamin as Jesus's was with Mary.

---

[35] John 20:16

Mary's rejoicing found her at the feet of Jesus in worship, bathed in the light of a new day. Gone was the dark night of her soul. Hope that does not disappoint breathed new life into her. Her joy bubbled out as she ran to tell the disciples, "I've just seen Jesus. He is alive!"

Life! Jesus once said, "I am the resurrection and the life." His victory over the grave proved the truth of his words. Hallelujah! Jesus is no corpse, nor is he a gardener. He is the Savior, the Christ. He is LORD!

Resurrection, Joseph style, came in Egyptian clothes and led to new life in the land of Goshen. God surely delivered Jacob's family from death, just as he had Joseph. What's more, Jacob's family was reunited, no longer separated by sin, hatred, and bitterness!

Maybe Joseph and his brothers never saw Jesus like Abraham and Jacob had; there is no Scripture record if God did appear to them. Neither does Jesus come and chat with us as he did with Abraham. However, just as God was continually with Joseph, God is with us. Emmanuel, "God with us," is more than the Divine limited by human form. Emmanuel, through the Holy Spirit, is powerfully with all who believe. The God who delivered Mary from her demons remained with her all the rest of her life because of Jesus's resurrection. The God whose plans included Joseph and his brothers was with them in Egypt, with them in the wilderness, and is still with them even now, these many centuries later.

Even before Jesus was born, there was resurrection. Just ask Joseph's brothers. God sent Joseph before them to preserve their lives. And God sent Jesus before us to save our lives. Can you hear Joseph's words in Jesus's invitation to us? "Come near to me, I pray you. I am Jesus. I am the resurrection and the life!"

This is good news! Let the reunion begin! Think resurrection, Joseph style. Amen, and thanks be to God!

Glossary

Lord – Yahweh. God revealed himself to Moses as I AM Who I AM in Exodus 3:14. When Scripture writes Lord with small capitals, it is referring to this personal name of God. The common term lord without the small capitals means master. (For example, Sarah called Abraham her lord, meaning her master—but certainly not her God!) It is much like how we use capitals to distinguish between god and God—god with a lowercase g is the generic form, and can mean any god or so-called god, while God with a capital G indicates God Himself, The Only True God. In many instances, Scripture refers to God as master, and uses the term Lord (with a capital L, out of reverence, just like using a capital G for God) to do so. But in some cases, Scripture is specifically referring to God's personal name, Yahweh, and when this happens, it records it as Lord (small capitals) to signify the difference. Joseph knew the I AM presence of the Lord, his God, the one who was and is and always will be. I have used small capitals throughout this book to indicate this name of God.

Joseph – My hero! The extraordinary son of Jacob and Rachel. Read all about him in Genesis 35–50.

Jacob – Joseph's dad was the son of Isaac and Rebekah. He was the father of twelve sons and one named daughter. Jacob was a man who learned to trust God's presence and guidance.

Esau – Jacob's twin brother, the firstborn. See Genesis 25:19–28:9.

Laban – Joseph's conniving grandfather was the father of Joseph's mother, Rachel (and her sister, Leah). Laban was also Joseph's grandmother Rebekah's brother.

Paddan-Aram – This highland plain is also known as Mesopotamia, the original home of the Hebrews (Genesis 11 and Acts 7:2).

Canaan – Canaan, a grandson of Noah (Genesis 9:18), left his mark on the land God promised to Abraham. As a territory, Canaan is first mentioned in Genesis 11:31. See Genesis 17:1–8 for more on God's promise to Joseph's great grandfather, Abraham.

Promised Land – Joseph's family left Egypt after four hundred thirty years there. Moses reminded the people of God's promise to give them a land flowing with milk and honey as they journeyed through the wilderness. Read Deuteronomy 6:3 and many other references, including Joshua 23:5, Psalm 47:4 (one of my favorites), and Hebrews 11:8–9.

Abraham – Joseph's great grandfather was known as a friend of God for his trust and godly obedience.

Ishmaelites – Abraham's firstborn, Ishmael, was the father of twelve sons. This band of brothers was known by their father's name as were Joseph and his brothers (Israelites).

Potiphar – Captain of the guard for Pharaoh and the owner of a slave named Joseph (Genesis 37:36). God blessed Potiphar and his household because Joseph was there (Genesis 39:5).

Abimelech – The King of Gerar (as seen in Genesis 20) was a man of integrity. Perhaps our hero, Joseph, had heard of this in the stories about Abraham and Sarah when they lived in Gerar.

Sarah – Abraham's wife gave birth to Isaac when she was 90! Nothing is too hard for the LORD (Genesis 17:17, 18:14, and 21:1–6).

Gerar – Joseph's grandparents, Isaac and Rebekah, like Isaac's father and mother, Abraham and Sarah, lived for a time in the land of Gerar (Genesis 20 and 26). This land was outside the land of Canaan, opposite Sodom and Gomorrah. Abraham went there after God destroyed the wicked cities (Genesis 10:19 and chapters 19 and 20).

Joshua – The right hand man for Moses and second in command until Moses's death, Joshua led Joseph's extended family into the land God promised Abraham. Joshua was a man who got his courage and strength from studying God's law. Be strong and courageous!

James – James was a brother of Jesus and the author of a New Testament letter bearing his name. James knew suffering, not unlike Joseph.

Job – Like Joseph, this faithful man suffered. Although his losses were overwhelming, Job still trusted God. A whole book of the Old Testament tells Job's story.

Chief Jailer – This keeper of the prison under Potiphar's command favored Joseph by putting him in charge of all the other prisoners. As you read Genesis 39:21–23, you can see how he trusted Joseph's leadership.

Moses – Like Joseph, Moses was rescued from almost certain death to become a deliverer. His story begins in Exodus 2.

Asher – One of Jacob's two sons to Leah's maid, Zilpah, and the eighth of Jacob's sons (Genesis 30:13).

Leah – Laban's older daughter and Jacob's first wife (an unwelcome wedding night bride exchange, a trick of Laban—Genesis 29:20–27). Leah bore Jacob six sons and one daughter: Reuben, Simeon, Levi, Judah, Issachar, Zebulun, and Dinah.

Emmanuel – Another name for Jesus (also spelled Immanuel), this name means God with us. Emmanuel is both the Person and the Presence Joseph knew well. Read Matthew 1:23 and Isaiah 7:14

Isaiah – Messenger and prophet who pointed the Israelites and Joseph's descendants to the coming Messiah, Christ, the Lord.

Israel – Another name for Jacob, won in his all-night wrestling match with God (Genesis 32:22–32). Israel was also the name of Jacob's descendants.

Pharaoh – Title of Egypt's kings. Senusret II ruled from 1897–1878 BC. Some scholars suggest he was the pharaoh during Joseph's time, although other scholars place Joseph in the 1700s BC.

Cupbearer – An Egyptian officer assigned to taste and serve the pharaoh his wine. In the event of poisoned drink, he would die to protect the king.

Baker – An Egyptian officer who tasted and served the king's food. In the event of poisoning, he would give his life in service to the pharaoh.

Jesus – Born of a woman, Jesus is God in the flesh. His divinity assures us that God is with us. His humanity comforts us that God understands what we go through. Jesus and Joseph have much in common. See the "Joseph and Jesus in Scripture" chart in the book for some of their similarities.

Samaria – The capital city of Israel, Samaria was purchased by King Omri (1 Kings 16:24). Samaria was the home of the woman who encountered Jesus at Joseph's well, according to John 4:5.

John (the beloved) – This Apostle was close to Jesus and he recorded Jesus's earthly experiences somewhat like a reporter on a mission. John's mission was revealed in John 20:35 and 21:24.

Sychar – The setting for Jesus's encounter with a Samaritan woman (John 4:5) on a parcel of land that once belonged to Joseph. Another name for this setting is Shechem, also known as Samaria.

Samaritan – A resident of Samaria, detested by the Jews and considered a half-breed (children born to American servicemen in the Korean conflict can relate).

Rachel – Joseph's mom, Rachel, was Jacob's beloved wife. She died while giving birth to Benjamin, Jacob's youngest child.

Prodigal Son – Luke 15 provides several parables or stories about being lost in ways that only Jesus could tell. Jesus told the story of the lost (prodigal) son in order to create pathways for being found and for life! Joseph's story is a prime example from of old.

Isaac – Jacob's father—the promised son of Abraham and Sarah. His name in Hebrew means laughter (compare Genesis 21:6 and Genesis 18:12).

Ishmael – Son of Abraham and Hagar (Sarah's maid). Ishmael, like Jacob, had twelve sons whose descendants continually clashed with the Israelites. (Modern Muslims trace their lineage to Ishmael, and continue to clash with the Jews!)

Paul – A once zealous Christian-killer, Paul encountered Jesus and became an ardent follower. To read his miraculous story, turn to Acts 7:57–8:3 and Acts 9:1–19.

David – Do you remember Joseph's brother Judah? He was the brother who fathered twin sons by his daughter-in-law, Tamar. His messed-up story is in Genesis 38. Eleven generations later, his descendant, David, son of Jesse, became king. David was a giant killer and a man after God's own heart. You can read all about it in 1 Samuel 13:14, 16:13, 17:12, 2 Samuel 5:12, and Acts 13:22.

The Chronicler – An unidentified individual (some believe it was Ezra the priest) who compiled documents to record David's role in and the centrality of the worship of God for the Israelites.

Ark of God – 1 Chronicles 15 records the move of the symbol of God's Presence to Jerusalem during David's reign. The Ark (also known as the Ark of the Covenant) was constructed in Moses' day according to God's command. It reminded Joseph's family that God was with them as they journeyed through the wilderness toward the Promised Land. When the Ark came to Jerusalem there was great rejoicing (see 1 Chronicles 16).

City of David – Headquarters for King David, the city ultimately became modern day Jerusalem in Israel. David captured the city from the Jebusites (2 Sam 7–9). As if to confuse us, Bethlehem is also known as the City of David. This was the birthplace of David and of his father Jesse—and also of Jesus (because his step-father, Joseph, was of the line of David, Luke 2:4).

Obed-edom – This man, a Gittite (a Canaanite tribe, not to be confused with Hittites), received unexpected blessings when his threshing floor became the temporary home of the Ark of the Covenant. Read about him in 1 Chronicles 13:13–14.

Levites – Priests descended from Jacob's son Levi.

Asaph – A Chief Priest, one of the Levites charged with worship during the reign of King David (1 Chronicles 16:4–5). In an interesting play on words, Asaph collected songs for worship, and his name means gatherer.

Michal – Daughter of Israel's first king, Saul. She was a wife of King David who despised David's worshipful dance (1 Chronicles 15:29).

Ezra – This Ezra was a descendant of Aaron, brother of Moses. He was a priest who knew the teachings of Moses by heart (Ezra 7:6). I call him a man of the Word. Ezra studied God's law and taught his fellow Israelites to do the same thing. The temple, destroyed by King Nebuchadnezzar, was rebuilt during Ezra's watch.

Babylon – Joseph's family struggled to stay faithful to God. The wise, the wealthy, and the influential among them were carried into exile by King Nebuchadnezzar of Babylon in 597BC.

Jerusalem – Once known as the City of David, Jerusalem became the holiest city for Joseph's kin with the placement of the Ark of God in her midst and subsequent Temple that housed it.

Salvation – Salvation for Joseph's family was provision—food in Egypt. Nourished bodies spared them the ravages of famine by God's design through the wisdom He supplied to Joseph. Salvation from the ravages of sin (the wages of sin is death according to Romans 6:23) comes by God's design through the death and resurrection of Jesus. Jesus called himself the Bread of Life in John 6:35. God's plan for life comes as we humble ourselves, like Joseph's brothers did, and ask for this eternal food in Christ Jesus.

Savior – A savior is one who rescues or redeems. Although Joseph was a savior for his family and the Egyptians in his care, only Jesus can save eternally.

Bethel – The word means House of God. The place, formerly known as Luz, was the site of Jacob's encounter with God in Genesis 35:1–7.

Pittsburghese – Pennsylvania dialect of those living in or near Pittsburgh. "Yinz might want to redd up your kitchen before company comes."

Mary and Joseph – Mother and step-father of Jesus. This Joseph was a carpenter by trade and was astonishing in his obedience to God through filling the role of Jesus's father on earth. Like our hero, he, too, was no ordinary Joe!

Judah – Jacob's fourth son—Joseph's brother, and an ancestor of Jesus.

Absalom – 2 Samuel 3:3 tells us that Absalom was David's third son. He deceitfully wrested David's throne from the King, but died by the spear as his tangled hair left him hanging in a tree. Read his sad story in 2 Samuel 14–19.

Manasseh – Joseph's firstborn son, whose name means causing to forget helped Joseph forget his past (Genesis 41:51).

Ephraim – Joseph's second son, whose name means fruitful, became a promise of fruitfulness for Joseph, despite all he had endured (Genesis 41:52).

Asenath – Joseph's wife was the daughter of Potiphera, an Egyptian priest (Genesis 41:45).

Benjamin – Joseph's youngest and only full blood brother was the second son of Rachel, who died in childbirth. Jacob named his youngest son Benjamin, which means son of the (or my) right hand (Genesis 35:16–20).

Perez – Firstborn son of Judah by Tamar and twin brother of Zerah (Genesis 38:27–29).

Zerah – Twin brother of Perez, born with a scarlet cord on his wrist! Read his story in Genesis 38:27–30.

Simeon – Joseph's next-to-the-oldest brother. Simeon had a quick temper and could be violent, as you can see in Genesis 34:5–7, 25–26.

Reuben – As Jacob's firstborn son, Reuben was Joseph's secret supporter. Read about it in Genesis 29:31-32 and Genesis 37:21–22.

Levi – Jacob's third son (Levi's mother was Leah). Levi's descendants eventually became the tribe of priests charged with worship. Levi means affection.

Bilhah – Rachel's maidservant, given to Jacob to bear sons in Rachel's name. Those sons were Dan and Naphtali (Genesis 30:1–8).

Dan – Joseph's brother and Jacob's fifth son (Genesis 30:4–6).

Naphtali – Jacob's sixth son, the younger of Bilhah's two sons (Genesis 30:7–8).

Zilpah – Leah's maidservant. Zilpah bore two sons: Gad and Asher were Jacob's seventh and eighth sons, respectively (Genesis 30:9–13).

Gad – Joseph's seventh brother. His mother was Zilpah. Gad means good fortune (Genesis 30:9–11).

Issachar – Joseph's ninth brother was Leah's son, her fifth of six boys (Genesis 30:17–18).

Zebulun – Leah's sixth and last son was Joseph's tenth brother. His name means honor or gift (Genesis 30:19–20).

Dinah – Jacob's only named daughter was Dinah, born between Zebulun and Joseph (Genesis 30:21–22).

Red Sea miracle – When it was time for Joseph's family to leave Egypt, the Egyptian army chased the nation-sized family to the sea. God blew back the waters and the people crossed on dry ground (Exodus 14:5–21)!

Deborah – A judge of Israel. Part commander and part spiritual leader after Joshua died, judges filled the Moses-shaped void. As a woman, Deborah was unusual in the role of judge, as was her victory over Sisera, a Canaanite king (Judges 4).

Ruth – Ruth was a Moabite girl who married into the Israelite family. She made their God her own God and became King David's great grandmother (Ruth 1–4).

Aaron – Moses's brother was a man who served as Moses's spokesman and a priest of God (Exodus 14:14–16 and Exodus 28:1).

Hur – Hur and Aaron helped Moses keep his hands lifted in prayer—not an easy task! Read Exodus 17 for the full story.

Goliath – This Philistine giant had the nerve to taunt God in front of "little" David. One smooth stone from David's slingshot (and the power of God!) toppled all nine feet of the man. 1 Samuel 17 fills in the details.

Er – Judah's firstborn. Er was the oldest of three sons to Judah's Canaanite wife. Er's wickedness caused his death and left his wife, Tamar, childless (Genesis 38:1–7).

Onan – Judah's second born rebelled against tradition (see Deuteronomy 25:5–10 for the custom that became law) and refused to father a son in Er's name. He died as a result (see Genesis 38:6–10).

Tamar – Joseph's brother Judah unwittingly impregnated his daughter-in-law, Tamar, after refusing to allow his youngest son, Shelah, to marry her. That God uses Tamar's twisted tale for good is evidence of amazing grace. Read more in Genesis 38 and Matthew 1:1–3 to watch Tamar go from victim to heroine.

Shelah – This son of Judah was a half-breed. His mother was the daughter of Shua of Adullam, a Canaanite. By rights, Shelah should have married Tamar, the widow of his brother Er. His story in Genesis 38:1–11 is messy, hiding nothing.

Goshen – This fertile land in Egypt became home to Jacob's family during the great seven-year famine when Joseph's leadership saved Egyptians and Israelites from starvation (see Genesis 47:1–12).

Canaanites – Residents of the land God promised to Abraham and his descendants were named for their ancestor, Canaan. Canaan was the son of Ham. Canaan's grandfather was Noah (Genesis 9:18 and Genesis 10:6).

Amos – A prophet of God about 753 years before the birth of Christ. Amos was a man who did not shrink under the charge to admonish God's people to repent of their sins. His prophecies cover the nine chapters of the Old Testament book bearing his name.

Rebekah – Joseph's paternal grandmother was the daughter of Abraham's brother Nahor. You can read her amazing story in Genesis 24.

Hittites – Ephron was a son of Heth, a Hittite (descendants of Noah's son Ham). Hittites owned the land Joseph's great-grandfather, Abraham, purchased as a burial place for Sarah. Joshua reminded Joseph's descendants of God's promise to give them the whole Canaanite territory, including the land of the Hittites, in Joshua 3:10 (compare with Exodus 3:8 and Joshua 24:11).

Machpelah – This cave was the family burial plot for Joseph's ancestors. His great-grandfather Abraham bought the field with this cave as a burial place when Sarah died. It was the only family-owned property in the Promised Land until the fulfillment of God's promise (Genesis 12:7 and Genesis 23).

Mary – Jesus delivered this Mary from seven demons (Luke 8:2). We call her Mary Magdalene because she came from the town of Magdala. As you might imagine, Mary became a devoted follower of Jesus and was among the women who hoped to properly anoint his body with burial spices on the first day of the week after his death (Luke 24:1 and John 20:1).

Integrity – Integrity is finishing a project or standing up for what you believe. Joseph's integrity kept him true to God while enslaved in Egypt; it helped him to love his brothers despite their betrayal. Integrity was a thread of character woven through Joseph's life and experience. It matters. It is possible. Just ask Joseph!

Works Cited

Card, Michael. *They Called Him Laughter (Isaac)*. Chatsworth, CA: N. Putman, 1989. Audio cassette.

Gilbreth, Jr., Frank and Carey, Ernestine Gilbreth. *Cheaper by the Dozen*. N.d. Kindle Edition.

Hawkins, O. S. *The Joshua Code*. Nashville: Thomas Nelson Publishers, 2012.

Joseph: King of Dreams, directed by Robert Ramirez and Rob LaDuca (2000; Dreamworks Animation), DVD.

Khan, Rana Rais. "Hospitality in Islam in Hiba: Enriching Lives," Volume 2, Issue 3 (November 12, 2012): http://www.hibamagazine.com/?s=hospitality+in+islam.

Merriam-Webster OnLine, s.v. "blessing," accessed July 15, 2014, http://www.merriam-webster.com/dictionary/blessing.

Morgan, Robert J. *The Promise: God Works All Things Together for Your Good*. Nashville: B & H Publishing Group, 2010.

Saint John of the Cross. *Dark Night of the Soul*. Christian Classics Ethereal Library (1994): http://www.ccel.org/ccel/john_cross/dark_night.html.

Schulman, Miriam and Amal Barkouki-Winter. "The Extra Mile in Markkula Center for Applied Ethics," Volume 11, Number 1 (Winter 2000): http://www.scu.edu/ethics/publications/iie/v11n1/hospitality.html.

Sweet, Leonard. *11 Indispensable Relationships You Can't Be Without.* Colorado Springs: David C. Cook, 2012.

Sweet, Leonard and Frank Viola. *Jesus: A Theography.* Nashville: Thomas Nelson, 2012. Kindle Edition.

Swindoll, Charles R. *Joseph: A Man of Integrity and Forgiveness.* Nashville: Word Publishing, 1998.